Canine Breed & Sport Guide

Dog Breed Traits
Plus
Sports Information & Precautions

Lost Temple Pets

Karen Cutler: LPTA, ACE Certified Personal Trainer

Canine Fitness/Nutrition & Canine Arthritis Management Practitioner *(CAMP)*

It is advised that you always check with your veterinarian before starting an exercise program or change in diet.

Websites

LostTempleFitness.com

LostTempleFitnessCancer.com

LostTemplePets.com

BREED GUIDE - TOC

CANINE SPORTS/ACTIVITIES - TOC

Introduction to Breed Charts

Dogs come in so many different sizes, temperaments and activity needs that it is hard to find everything you want in one package. They were bred for many different reasons from hunting to sledding to protection to just plain companionship. Dogs have come so far from the wild dogs in Africa and wolves to the pugs we see today. There are over 160 AKC registered dogs, not to mention the designer dogs, such as puggles and many lovable mutts, which can be the best of many mixtures. How do you know which ones will fit into your active lifestyle or sport you wish to participate in? The purpose of this guide is to *help* pinpoint that decision down to at least 5-10 possible choices out of 160+ AKC registered breeds, and then you can continue your research on endless numbers of web sites and books.

First you have to decide what sport or activity you would like to be involved with. If you are an active person, sports such as Canicross, Agility or Disc Dog may be the thing for you. Just keep in mind that if you pick a border collie or Belgian Malinois, these dogs are active *all* the time, not just on the weekends. If you want your companion to do all the work, then Earthdog, Weight Pulling or Lure Coursing may be the thing for you - although dogs that enter these sports need plenty of exercise outside the competitions.

This book will help you find the perfect pet to fit your lifestyle based on:

- *Size*
- *What the dog was bred to do*
- *Activity level*
- *Exercise needs*
- *OFA Suggested Orthopedic testing, if adopting a purebred puppy*
- *Body Type*
- *Sport or Activity the breed 'usually' excels at*
- *Other helpful information about what makes each breed unique*

Keep in mind that this is a guide based on standard personalities. You may get a Golden Retriever that has no interest in the game of go-fetch. It is important to test the dog or puppy before buying. If the puppy has no interest retrieving when he is at the shelter or breeder, he will have no interest when you get him home. On the flip side, I have seen Corgi's win Agility competitions. If you are buying a breed that has history of hip dysplasia, be careful to make sure the breeder has certified that the line is free of this arthritic condition.

WORKING DOG AS PETS Some breeds of dogs need to keep busy. If you are going to get a working canine as a companion, such as a Border Collie or German Shepherd, know that these dogs can get very destructive if not given a job to do. These breeds also need to be exercised on a regular basis physically, as well as challenged mentally. Before purchasing, know what the dog was bred to do, and then decide if they will fit into your lifestyle. You may not want a Border Collie to herd sheep, but you may want a dog that excels in agility trials, treibball or disc dog. If you have other small pets at home, keep in mind that a border collie may try to herd (chase) the cat.

SHOW/PET VS. WORKING LINES: When choosing a working, herding, sporting or hound dog as a pet, check whether the dog was bred for show or work. There may be differences in size, temperament and focus. On the other hand, if you are looking for a hunting dog, you want to purchase a dog from a breeder that specializes in selective breeding for this purpose.

Do your research before going to a shelter or a breeder and know what you are looking for before you go through that door. Also keep in mind that unlike some other pets, dogs are very social animals and will not be happy being by themselves for long periods of time, especially as a puppy. Consider your own lifestyle not only now, but in the future, before committing to adopting a dog.

That puppy you take home is only a puppy for a short amount of time. Be prepared to adopt or purchase a dog that will be with you up to 10-15+ years.

Dog Breed Chart

Chart Description

Arrangement of American Kennel Club (AKC) registered breeds by size:

Extra Small
Small
Medium
Large (includes Extra Large breeds)

<u>*Group:*</u>   Each breed is grouped together in 1 of 8 particular categories. *Descriptions have been quoted from the AKC Group Description (http://www.akc.org/breeds/index.cfm?nav_area=breeds#)*

Sporting*:*   **Naturally** active and alert, Sporting dogs make likeable, well-rounded companions. Members of the Group include pointers, retrievers, setters and spaniels. Remarkable for their instincts in water and woods, many of these breeds actively continue to participate in   hunting and other field activities. Potential owners of Sporting dogs need to realize that most require regular, invigorating exercise.

Hound: **Most** hounds share the common ancestral trait of being used for hunting. Some use acute scenting powers to follow a trail. Others demonstrate a phenomenal gift of stamina as they relentlessly run down quarry. Beyond this, however, generalizations about hounds are hard to come by, since the Group encompasses quite a diverse lot. There are Pharaoh Hounds, Norwegian Elkhounds, Afghans and Beagles, among others. Some hounds share the distinct ability to produce a unique sound known as baying. You'd best sample this sound before you decide to get a hound of your own to be sure it's your cup of tea.

Working: **Dogs** of the Working Group were bred to perform such jobs as guarding property, pulling sleds and performing water rescues. They have been invaluable assets to man throughout the ages. The Doberman pinscher, Siberian husky and Great Dane are included in this Group, to name just a few.
Quick to learn, these intelligent, capable animals make solid companions. Their considerable dimensions and strength alone, however, make many working dogs unsuitable
as pets for average families. By virtue of their size alone, these dogs must be properly trained.

Toy: **The diminutive** size and winsome expressions of Toy dogs illustrate the main function of this Group: to embody sheer delight. Don't let their tiny stature fool you, though - - many Toys are tough as nails. If you haven't yet experienced the barking of an angry Chihuahua, for example, well, just wait. Toy dogs will always be popular with city dwellers and people without much living space. They make ideal apartment dogs and terrific lap warmers on nippy nights. (Incidentally, small breeds may be found in every Group, not just the Toy Group. We advise everyone to seriously consider getting a small breed, when appropriate, if for no other reason than to minimize some of the problems inherent in canines such as shedding, creating messes and cost of care. And training aside, it's still easier to control a ten-pound dog than it is one ten times that size.)

Terrier: **People** familiar with this Group invariably comment on the distinctive terrier personality. These are feisty, energetic dogs whose sizes range from fairly small, as in the Norfolk, Cairn or West Highland white terrier, to the grand Airedale terrier. Terriers typically have little tolerance for other animals, including other dogs. Their ancestors were bred to hunt and kill vermin. Many continue to project the attitude that they're always eager for a spirited argument. Most terriers have wiry coats that require special grooming known as stripping in order to maintain a characteristic appearance. In general, they make engaging pets, but require owners with the determination to match their dogs' lively characters.

Non-Sporting: **Non-sporting** dogs are a diverse group. Here are sturdy animals with as different personalities and appearances as the Chow Chow, Dalmatian, French Bulldog, and Keeshond. Talk about differences in size, coat, and visage! Some, like the Schipperke and Tibetan spaniel are uncommon sights in the average neighborhood. Others, however, like the Poodle and Lhasa Apso, have quite a large following. The breeds in the Non-Sporting Group are a varied collection in terms of size, coat, personality and overall appearance.

Herding: **The Herding Group,** created in 1983, is the newest AKC classification; its members were formerly members of the Working Group. All breeds share the fabulous ability to control the movement of other animals. A remarkable example is the low-set Corgi, perhaps one foot tall at the shoulders that can drive a herd of cows many times its size to pasture by leaping and nipping at their heels. The vast majority of Herding dogs, as household pets, never cross paths with a farm animal. Nevertheless, pure instinct prompts many of these dogs to gently herd their owners, especially the children of the family. In general, these intelligent dogs make excellent companions and respond beautifully to training exercises.

Miscellaneous: **(Not listed)**   *(www.akc.org/breeds/index.cfm?nav_area=breeds#)*

Purpose: *What was the dog bred to do?*

Companion – Keep people company.
Watch Dog – Watch over property by barking, etc.
Guard Dog – Physically guard property, people or livestock.
Hunter – Hunt animals, such as rats, birds, vermin, wolves, foxes, etc.
Tracker – Track people or animals by scent.
Scent Hound – Hunt by scent.
Sight Hound – Hunt by sight.
Sled Dog – Pull sleds.
Bull Baiting – A sport where a bull was tied to an iron stake with a 30 ft. radius. The dog then had to immobilize the bull.

Size:

The average weight in pounds by AKC standards
The average height in inches at withers by AKC standards

Activity Level:

+++   Very active
++   Moderately active
+   Pretty laid back

Exercise Needs:

****   Needs lots of exercise. Needs room to run, as well as to be taken for long walks several times a day.
***   Needs exercise/walks, including small dogs that may need to be mentally stimulated if left in the house too long.
**   Needs exercise, although may be OK if they don't get out every day.
*   Although all dogs require exercise, these dogs may need a little 'push' to participate.

OFA – Suggested Orthopedic Tests – *Please see next section for link and complete description*

Elbow Dysplasia
Hip Dysplasia
Legg-Calve-Perthes Disease (LCP)
Patella Luxation

Body Types - *Please see next section for complete description of Body Types and Weight to Height Ratio*
Some sports depend on a dog's body type such as Ectomorphic, Mesomorphic, Endomorphic, Micromelic Achondroplasia, Ateliotic Pituitary Dwarf, Giants and Brachycephalic Achondroplasia.

Sport or Activity
These are breeds that are particularly good at a sport or activity. This does not mean that other dogs cannot participate, or may not excel at these activities. See Sports or Activity.

More information:
Extra information about each breeds personality.

Dog Aggressive: These dogs can be aggressive with other dogs, some mainly with same sex dogs. Early socialization will help to deter this at a later age.

Do not trust with non-canine pets: These dogs were bred as hunters and usually have a natural prey drive. Some can be alright with other animals if they are raised together.
For example, a terrier that was bred to hunt rats should probably not be left alone with the pet hamster.

Soft Mouthed – A dog that will carry prey without biting down.

Sports or Activity

For a more complete description, please refer to the 2nd section entitled *Sports and Activities,* which also includes contraindications for both you and your dog, equipment, training needs, commands, and more.

Agility
A sport in which the handler guides the dog through an obstacle course. The course is timed and points are deducted for faults, such as knocking a bar over or not correctly going through the weave poles.

Bikejoring
This is a recreation or sport where a harnessed dog or team of dogs attached to a towline, pull and run ahead or at the side of a cyclist. Bikejoring is also sometimes used to train racing sled-dogs out of season.

Bomb Detection
Special trained dogs that are trained to follow the scent of bombs or other explosive devices.

Canicross
This sport is also called cross country running with dogs. The runner wears a waist belt with 1 or 2 dogs attached. The dogs or dogs wear a harness and are placed in the front to pull the runner. The dogs are attached by a bungee type cord.

Carting
Larger dogs are usually used, as this competition usually involves pulling a cart with a person inside.

Disc dog or Frisbee dog
Disc dog is a competition where dogs and their human disc throwers compete in events such as distance catching and somewhat choreographed freestyle catching. The term "disc" is preferred because "Frisbee" is a trademark (held by Wham-O) for a brand of flying disc.

Dock Diving or Jumping
This is a competition where dogs, usually retrievers, are encouraged to jump off a dock into a body of water, such as a lake or pool. The dock itself is usually about 40 ft, although it is not necessary that the dog use the entire dock before jumping off. The jump distance is then measured. The owner may or may not use a toy or chase object to entice the dog into the water. (*wikipedia.org/wiki/Dock_diving*)

Dog or Pack Hiking
A form of hiking with your dog where the dog will carry a backpack fitted especially for dogs.

Dog Scootering
Similar to Bikejoring, this is a recreation or sport where one or two dogs pull a human riding an un-motorized kick scooter. The dogs wear the same harness that sled dogs wear, and are hooked to the scooter with a gangline.

Earth Dog Trials
This competition is intended for short-legged terriers. The dog must negotiate man-made tunnels to test the dog's ability to follow the scent and work the quarry.

Flyball
This is a sport that incorporates a team of dogs. It is basically a relay race in which dogs run over hurdles placed 10 feet apart for a total of 51 feet to get a tennis ball that is released from a box and return it to the start. At this point another dog takes over with a total of 4 dogs on each team. Flyball is also great for small breeds, as the hurdles are measured by the shortest dog on the team.

Guard Dog
These dogs have the physical ability to protect you or your property.

Herding, Sheep Trials or Stock Dog *(also see Sheepdog Trials)*
Herding can involve the dog luring various animals to get them across a field or in a pen. This can either be competitive trials or for livestock in farms/ranches.

Hunting
Breeds that tend to excel in hunting prey - these can include pointers, retrievers and trackers.

Jog
Dogs are ranked from No> OK > Good > Great in their ability to stay with you in an average paced jog. In no way does this mean that any dog should not be walked on a daily basis. See *Walking* below.

Lure Coursing
This is sport that is usually for sight hound breeds only, such as the Whippet, Saluki and Borzoi. The purpose is for these hounds to chase a fake lure across a field, usually between 600-1000 yards. The lure is meant to represent live prey and may include several turns.

Mushing
A general term for a sport or transport method powered by dogs, and includes carting, pulka, scootering, sled dog racing, skijoring, freighting, and weight pulling. More specifically, it implies the use of one or more dogs to pull a sled on snow.

Musical Canine Freestyle – *Also called musical freestyle, freestyle dance, and canine freestyle*
A modern dog sport that is a mixture of obedience, tricks, and dance that allows for creative interaction between dogs and their owners.

Narcotics Detection
Special trained dogs that are bred to follow the scent of narcotics.

Obedience
Competition where dogs are expected to follow commands by their handler - can be any dog, but some breeds are easier to train.

Performing Tricks
Breeds that learn easily and love to show off.

Pointing
Hunting dogs that are bred to point out game to the handler.

Racing
A sport where the canine chases a lure around a track to the finish line. The first dog to cross the finish line wins.

Retrievers
Competitions or for other sports that require the dog to bring back an article. This can be in hunting, dock diving or just for fun.

Ring Sport
A dog sport involving jumps, obedience, and bite work. This includes Belgian, Mondio and French. Similar to Schutzhund. .

Scootering – *See Dog Scootering*

Schutzhund
Developed in Germany to test a dog's physical and mental abilities that are necessary for police work. This competition tests strength, endurance, agility, tracking and obedience. Breeds usually seen in these competitions include German Shepherds, Belgian Shepherds, and Giant Schnauzers among others.

Sheepdog Trials
A competitive dog sport in which herding dog breeds move sheep around a field, fences, gates, or enclosures as directed by their handlers. Such events are particularly associated with hill farming areas, where sheep range widely on largely unfenced land. *(wikipedia.org/wiki/Sheepdog_trial)*

Skijoring -*with dog*
A sport in which one to three dogs assist a cross-country skier. The cross-country skier provides power with skis and poles, and the dog adds additional power by running and pulling. The skier wears a skijoring harness, which is connected to the dog wearing a sled dog harness. *(wikipedia.org/wiki/Skijoring)*

Sled Dog Racing
A winter sport where a group of 3-24 sled dogs are harnessed to a sled and run over a set course with the musher or dog driver standing on the runner. Sprint races can last up to 4-25 miles a day, mid distance 28-200 miles, and long distance from 200-1000 miles. *(wikipedia.org/wiki/Dogsled_racing)*

Therapy Dog
Dogs that tend to have a nurturing personality and are no easily frightened by a range of people. These dogs are brought into hospitals, nursing homes and other places to help lift spirits.

Tracking Trials
An event where dogs are encouraged to follow a scent trail. This could be for hunting purposes or searching for humans, articles or other items.

Watch Dog
These dogs tend to bark to protect their territory, whether it be home or human.

Weight pulling
A sport invented mainly for bull and sled pulling breeds. The dogs must pull a sled or cart loaded with weight across a set distance over grass, snow or carpet. The dog is hitched to a harness and then encouraged to pull the sled to a finish line. Although any dog can join this event, be careful of breeds like the Italian Greyhound and other fragile dogs that can easily fracture bones in their chest area.

Weiner Racing –*Also Dachshund Racing*
Typical races are either 25 or 50 yards in length, and are run on various surfaces. In the less formal events, most entrants are not career racers, nor bred for racing.

Swimming and Walking
The advantages of swimming are:
- On a regular basis, swimming can help build the endurance, muscle strength, flexibility, range of motion in joints and cardiovascular fitness.
- This is a great sport for all fitness levels.
- This can help in post surgery to avoid muscle atrophy and weakness. Swimming is also good for people and pets that cannot do weight bearing activities – it provides unloading on painful joints, and early weight bearing.
- Swimming does not put the strain on connective tissues that running, aerobics and some weight-training routines do.
- Hydrotherapy in an underwater treadmill helps the canine with limb extension, where swimming does more to help flexion.

The advantages of walking:
- Whether you live in the city or country, there is usually a place that you can walk.
- Improves cardiovascular fitness.
- Walking helps with weight loss.
- Walking with your dog helps to build up your endurance, as most dogs will be more than happy to walk as far as you can tolerate.
- Walking helps increase bone density.
- It is a great way to burn off energy for your dog. A tired dog is a happy dog.
- Change of scenery for both you and your dog.   Despite having a 'big' back yard or having a small dog in an apartment, most dogs get tired of looking at the same four walls. Walking your dog enhances their senses, helps them socially, and best of all gives them quality time with you. 30+ minutes a day also helps decrease depression in humans.

OFA – Suggested Orthopedic Tests

Please see individual links for more information on each condition or visit Lost Temple Pets website Arthritis & Orthopedic section - *https://losttemplepets.com/canine-arthritis-breeds-at-risk/*

Elbow Dysplasia – *https://ofa.org/diseases/elbow-dysplasia/*
Elbow dysplasia is a general term used to identify an inherited polygenic disease in the elbow. Three specific etiologies make up this disease and they can occur independently or in conjunction with one another. These etiologies include:

- Pathology involving the medial coronoid of the ulna (FCP)
- Osteochondritis of the medial humeral condyle in the elbow joint (OCD)
- Ununited anconeal process (UAP)

Studies have shown the inherited polygenic traits causing these etiologies are independent of one another. Clinical signs involve lameness which may remain subtle for long periods of time. No one can predict at what age lameness will occur in a dog due to a large number of genetic and environmental factors such as degree of severity of changes, rate of weight gain, amount of exercise, etc.. Subtle changes in gait may be characterized by excessive inward deviation of the paw which raises the outside of the paw so that it receives less weight and distributes more mechanical weight on the outside (lateral) aspect of the elbow joint away from the lesions located on the inside of the joint. Range of motion in the elbow is also decreased.

Hip Dysplasia – *https://ofa.org/diseases/hip-dysplasia/*
Canine Hip Dysplasia typically develops because of an abnormally developed hip joint, but can also be caused by cartilage damage from a traumatic fracture. With cartilage damage or a hip joint that isn't formed properly, over time the existing cartilage will lose its thickness and elasticity. This breakdown of the cartilage will eventually result in pain with any joint movement.

No one can predict when or even if a dysplastic dog will start showing clinical signs of lameness due to pain. The severity of the disease can be affected by environmental factors, such as caloric intake or level of exercise. There are a number of dysplastic dogs with severe arthritis that run, jump, and play as if nothing is wrong and some dogs with barely any arthritic x-ray evidence that are severely lame.

Legg-Calve-Perthes Disease (LCP) *https://ofa.org/diseases/other-phenotypic-evaluations/legg-calve-perthes/*
Legg-Calve-Perthes Disease (LCP) is a disorder of hip joint conformation occurring in both humans and dogs. In dogs, it is most often seen in the miniature and toy breeds between the ages of 4 months to a year.

LCP results when the blood supply to the femoral head is interrupted resulting in avascular necrosis, or the death of the bone cells. Followed by a period of revascularization, the femoral head is subject to remodeling and/or collapse creating an irregular fit in the acetabulum, or socket. This process of bone cells dying and fracturing followed by new bone growth and remodeling of the femoral head and neck, can lead to stiffness and pain. LCP is believed to be an inherited disease, although the mode of inheritance is not known. Because there is a genetic component, it is recommended that dogs affected with LCP not be used in breeding programs.

Patellar Luxation *https://ofa.org/diseases/patellar-luxation/*
The patella, or kneecap, is part of the stifle joint (knee). In patellar luxation, the kneecap luxates, or pops out of place, either in a medial or lateral position.

Bilateral involvement is most common, but unilateral is not uncommon. Animals can be affected by the time they are eight weeks of age. The most notable finding is a knock-knee (genu valgum) stance. The patella is usually reducible, and laxity of the medial collateral ligament may be evident. The medial retinacular tissues of the stifle joint are often thickened, and the foot can be seen to twist laterally as weight is placed on the limb.
Patellar luxations fall into several categories:

1. Medial luxation (toy, miniature, and large breeds)
2. Lateral luxation (toy and miniature breeds)
3. Lateral luxation (large and giant breeds)
4. Luxation resulting from trauma (various breeds, of no importance to the certification process)

WEIGHT-TO-HEIGHT RATIO & BODY TYPE

HUMAN

In most sports long limbs does have its advantages, including basketball, tennis, soccer and running. This is due to longer levers in the extremities, as well as height. In the human body, bones act as levers.

- The axis of a bone passes through a joint and it is moved by muscle forces (the effort) at the point of muscle attachment. The load consists of any resistance to movement.
- Sports implements, such as golf clubs and rackets, become levers when held in the hand. The usual function of a lever is to gain a <u>mechanical advantage</u>, whereby a small force applied over a large distance at one end of the lever produces a greater force operating over a smaller distance at the other end of the lever, or whereby a given speed of movement at one end of the lever is greatly increased at the other end. This gives an advantage in both humans and canines when it comes to jumping, running, kicking or hitting.

On the other hand, when it comes to strength, because of a shorter lever arm, being compact has its advantages. This is known in power-lifting, gymnastics and amateur wrestling. In canine weight pulling it may be advantageous to be on the short side, as you will need to be near the ground to entice your dog over the finish line.

Luckily, when it comes to most canine sports, average is OK. Agility, dancing, disc dog and mushing, among many others, really don't take height into consideration. On the other hand, staying at a healthy weight will help in all sports, canine or otherwise - unless you are a Sumo wrestler.

CANINE

The heavier the dog, the more stress is put on the musculoskeletal system in regards to jumping and agility type sports.

- If the dog is tall, but heavy he will have more trouble getting off the ground and have to put more effort into locomotion.
- A lighter breed at the same height will be putting less stress on the musculoskeletal system. An Australian shepherd at 42 lbs., 20 in. high and a basset hound at 45 lbs., 11 in. high, although similar in weight, are not going to be able to jump the same distance. The basset hound carries the same weight on shorter legs/frame and would have to increase the effort in his jump compared to the Australian shepherd.

The smaller the ratio, the better they will be in agility type sports.

- A Papillon at 7 lbs., 11 inches tall has a weight/height ratio of 0.6
- A Bull mastiff at 135 lbs., 26 inches tall has a weight/height ratio of 5.2

Larger breeds like the mastiff are better at weight pulling competitions where they will not put stress on their joints with repetitive jumping. Although many dogs can do weight pulling, it is advised that dogs with fragile bones like the Italian greyhound do not participate in this sport.

- It is just as important to keep your border collie at a healthy weight to decrease the stress on the front end when landing, and the effort it takes to jump in agility. *(Zink and Daniels, 2005, p. 5-6)*

BODY TYPES and EXAMPLES

Body Types	Canine	Canine Sport	Human Sport

Ectomorphic:
Tall
Long Limbs
Light boned
	Sight-hound
	Example
	  Greyhound
	  Saluki
		Lure coursing
		Agility
		Racing
			Running
			Basketball

Mesomorphic:
Medium Build
Moderate boned
Well-muscled
	Retriever
	Herding
	Example
	  Golden Retriever
	  German Shepherd
		Most any sport
		Flyball
		Agility
			Most any sport
			Running
			Sprinting
			Weightlifting
			Hockey

Endomorphic:
Average/Large size
Heavy Boned
	Bull type dogs
	Example
	  Mastiffs
	  Bull Terrier
		Weight pulling
		Cart Pulling
			Power lifting
			Football

Micromelic Achondroplasia
Short Limbs
Relatively normal bodies
(may be slightly elongated)
	Example
	  Corgis
	  Dachshund
		Breed specific	

Ateliotic Pituitary Dwarf:
Small, but relatively equal body/leg size
	Example
	  Maltese
	  Chihuahua
		Agility	

Giants
Larger size
Can be ecto., meso., or endo.
	Example
	  Irish Wolfhound (ecto)
	  Great Dane (meso)
	  St. Bernard (endo)
		Breed specific	

Brachycephalic Achondroplasia Shorted Bones of the Skull	*Example* Pug English Bull Dog	Precaution with activity in the heat	

EXTRA SMALL – LARGE DOG BREED CHARTS

Extra Small **Breed**	Group / Purpose for breeding	Size Lbs. Ht./inch	Activity Level+ ---------- Exercise Needs*	Suggested Orthopedic OFA Tests	Body Type	Sport or Activity	Information
Affenpinscher	*Group:* Toy *Purpose:* Hunter Ratter	7-10 lbs. 11 inch	+++ **	Hip Dysplasia Legg-Calve-Perthes Patella Luxation	Ateliotic Pituitary Dwarf Brachycephalic	Agility Jog - OK Performing Tricks Watch Dog	'Monkey Dog'. *Can be Dog Aggressive* Active, adventurous, stubborn, curious, playful, confident, protective, difficult to housebreak, can become bored, fearless *Difficult to breed usually requiring cesarean section*
Brussels Griffon	*Group:* Toy *Purpose:* Hunter Ratter	8-10 lbs. 8 inch	+++ **	Hip Dysplasia Patella Luxation	Ateliotic Pituitary Dwarf Brachycephalic	Agility Jog - OK Performing Tricks Watch Dog	Huge heart, high strung, emotionally sensitive, demanding, alert, full of self-importance, inquisitive, dominates larger dogs, likes to snuggle *Difficult to breed usually requiring cesarean section*
Chihuahua	*Group:* Toy *Purpose:* Companion	2-6 lbs. 8-9 inch	++ **	Patella Luxation	Ateliotic Pituitary Dwarf	Watch Dog Jog - No	*Can be Dog Aggressive* Bold, strong-willed, can snap at children, protective, demands attention, can be dog aggressive, devoted *Smallest breed of dog in the world. Also bred in a smaller teacup version* *Gets cold easily* *Bred in both long hair and short hair*

Extra Small Breed	Group Purpose for breeding	Size Lbs. Ht./ inch	Activity Level+ ----------- Exercise Needs*	Suggested Orthopedic OFA Tests	Body Type	Sport or Activity	Information
Italian Greyhound	**Group:** Hound **Purpose:** Companion Sight-hound	8 lbs. 13-15 inch	+++ **	Hip Dysplasia Legg-Calve-Perthes Patellar Luxation	Ateliotic Pituitary Dwarf Ectomorphic	Jog - Good Racing Watch Dog	Good w/ kids/pets when raised together, extremely fast, gentle, submissive, high strung, timid, good family dog, high prey drive, mischievous, can walk upright, agile, athletic, does not like cold weather, eating is sporadic, lack of bladder control, use harness instead of collar *Smallest sight hound* *Fragile – Does not do well playing rough*
Japanese Chin	**Group:** Toy **Purpose:** Companion	7 lbs. 9 inch	++ **	Patella Luxation	Ateliotic Pituitary Dwarf Micromelic Achondroplasia Brachycephalic	Agility Jog - OK Performing Tricks Therapy Dog Watch Dog	Lively, mild mannered, sensitive, agile, cat-like, uses paws to wash face, alert, independent *Prefers familiar surroundings* *Developed in Japan, often given as gifts*
Maltese	**Group**: Toy **Purpose:** Companion	7 lbs. 7-9 inch	+++ **	Patella Luxation	Ateliotic Pituitary Dwarf	Jog - OK Obedience Training Performing Tricks Watch Dog	Lively, playful, trusting learns tricks easily, likes to chase and run, may be hard to housebreak *Prone to sunburn and tear stains under eyes*
Manchester Terrier (Toy) AKA Rat Terrier	**Group:** Toy **Purpose:** Hunter Ratter	12 lbs. 10-12 inch	+++ **	Legg-Calve-Perthes Patella Luxation	Ateliotic Pituitary Dwarf	Agility Jog - OK Watch Dog	*Can be Dog Aggressive Not good with non-canine pets or children* Headstrong, protective, active, good with the elderly, likes to chase *Fragile – Does not do well playing rough*

Extra Small **Breed**	*Group* *Purpose for breeding*	<u>Size</u> Lbs. Ht./ inch	Activity Level+ ---------- *Exercise Needs**	Suggested Orthopedic OFA Tests	**Body Type**	*Sport or Activity*	*More Information*
Miniature Pincher (Min Pin)	*Group:* Toy *Purpose:* Hunter Ratter	8-10 lbs. 10-12.5 inch	+++ **	Legg-Calve-Perthes Patella Luxation	Ateliotic Pituitary Dwarf	Agility Jog - OK Obedience Training Watch Dog	*Can be Dog Aggressive.* Fearless, proud, very energetic, headstrong, independent, hardy breed, territorial, use harness instead of collar
Norfolk Terrier	*Group:* Terrier *Purpose:* Hunter Vermin Fox	11-12 lbs. 9-10 inch	+++ **	Hip Dysplasia Patella Luxation	Ateliotic Pituitary Dwarf	Agility Hunting Jog - OK Tracking Watch Dog	Hard to housebreak, likes to dig, devoted, outgoing, brave, independent *Work well in a pack*
Norwich Terrier	*Group:* Terrier *Purpose:* Hunter Vermin Fox	11-12 lbs. 10 inch	+++ **	Hip Dysplasia Patella Luxation	Ateliotic Pituitary Dwarf	Agility Hunting Jog - OK Tracking Watch Dog	Hard to housebreak, likes to dig, devoted, outgoing, brave, independent *Work well in a pack*
Papillon	*Group:* Toy *Purpose:* Companion	5-11 lbs. 8-11 inch	++ **	Patella Luxation	Ateliotic Pituitary Dwarf	Agility Jog - OK Obedience Training Performing Tricks Watch Dog	*Can be slightly Dog Aggressive* Gentle, affectionate, calm, patient, can be difficult to housebreak, jealous, likes to cuddle, hardy, very energetic *Was popular with royal courts and aristocrats*
Pekingese	*Group:* Toy *Purpose:* Companion	14 lbs. 8 inch	++ **	No Information Available	Ateliotic Pituitary Dwarf Micromelic Achondroplasia Brachycephalic	Jog - No Watch Dog	Can be snappy, sweet, loyal, affectionate, loving, gets bored with repetition, willful rambunctious *Bred to resemble Chinese Foo Dogs, thought to keep away evil spirits. Also named Sleeve Pekingese , which came from the custom of carrying them in the sleeves of robes worn by members of the Chinese Imperials*

Extra Small *Breed*	**Group** Purpose for breeding	Size Lbs. Ht./ inch	Activity Level+ ---------- Exercise Needs*	Suggested Orthopedic OFA Tests	Body Type	Sport or Activity	More Information
Pomeranian	*Group:* Toy *Purpose:* Companion	3-7 lbs. 7-12 inch	++ **	Hip Dysplasia Patellar Luxation	Ateliotic Pituitary Dwarf	Agility Jog - No/OK Performing Tricks Watch Dog	Can be Dog Aggressive Willful, bold, temperamental, curious, protective of owner, playful, active
Poodle, Toy	*Group:* Toy *Purpose:* Hunter Companion	6 lbs. 10 inch	+++ **	Patellar Luxation	Ateliotic Pituitary Dwarf	Agility Jog - OK Obedience Training Performing Tricks Retrieving Watch Dog	Extremely intelligent, trainable, pleasant, happy, clever, reserved with strangers, can 'understand speech' Has also been used to sniff out truffles One of the most intelligent and trainable breeds (See Poodle, Miniature under Small for more info)
Shih Tzu	*Group:* Toy *Purpose:* Companion	9-18 lbs. 8-11 inch	++ **	Hip Dysplasia Patellar Luxation	Ateliotic Pituitary Dwarf Brachycephalic	Jog - OK Watch Dog	'Lion Dog', Difficult to housebreak, assertive, arrogant, proud, friendly, loyal, can be snappish, adaptable Do not overfeed Bred to be a companion dog for Chinese royalty
Silky Terrier AKA Australian Silky Terrier	*Group:* Toy *Purpose:* Companion Hunter Ratter	8-11 lbs. 9-10 inch	++ **	Patellar Luxation	Ateliotic Pituitary Dwarf	Agility Jog - OK Performing Tricks Watch Dog	Can Be Dog Aggressive Travels well, lively, can be stubborn, likes to be treated as an equal, alert, active, gets bored easily Over-sensitive to voice tones

Extra Small Breed	Group Purpose for breeding	Size Lbs. Ht./ inch	Activity Level+ ---------- Exercise Needs*	Suggested Orthopedic OFA Tests	Body Type	Sport or Activity	More Information
Tibetan Spaniel	*Group:* Non-Sporting *Purpose:* Watch Dog Companion	9-15 lbs. 10 inch	++ **	Patellar Luxation	Ateliotic Pituitary Dwarf Micromelic Achondroplasia Brachycephalic	Agility Jog - Good Performing Tricks Watch Dog	*Not a true spaniel* Happy, smart, trusting, insistent, aloof with strangers, assertive, highly intelligent *Likes to sit in high places* *Watch dog at Tibetan monasteries*
Toy Fox Terrier	*Group:* Toy *Purpose:* Hunter Ratter Companion	3-7 lbs. 9-11 inch	++ **	Legg-Calve-Perthes Patellar Luxation	Ateliotic Pituitary Dwarf	Agility Jog - OK Performing Tricks Therapy Dog Watch Dog	*Do not trust w/ non-canine pets* Not *as* active as some other terrier breeds, energetic, courageous, outgoing, friendly, sensitive to cold *Some are allergic to beet pulp, corn and wheat*
Yorkshire Terrier	*Group:* Toy *Purpose:* Hunter Ratter Companion	7 lbs. 7.5 inch	++ **	Hip Dysplasia Legg-Calve-Perthes Patellar Luxation	Ateliotic Pituitary Dwarf Brachycephalic	Agility Jog - OK Obedience Training Watch Dog	*Can be Dog Aggressive Do not trust w/ non-canine pets* Energetic, affectionate, independent, courageous, self-confident, bold, may be hard to housebreak

Small Breed	Group Purpose for breeding	Size Lbs. Ht./ inch	Activity Level+ ---------- Exercise Needs*	Suggested Orthopedic OFA Tests	Body Type	Sport or Activity	More Information
American Eskimo (Toy & Standard)	**Group:** Non-Sporting **Purpose:** Companion	Toy 6-10 lbs. 9-12 inch Standard 19-35 lbs. 16-21 inch	++ ***	Elbow Dysplasia Hip Dysplasia Legg-Calve-Perthes Patella Luxation	Ateliotic Pituitary Dwarf	Agility Jog - Good Narcotic Detection Obedience Training Performing Tricks Watch Dog	Intelligent, good with children, willful, protective, energetic, eager to please, very active Prone to separation anxiety
Australian Terrier	**Group:** Terrier **Purpose:** Companion Hunter Ratter Watchdog	12-14 lbs.. 10-11 inch	+++ **	Patellar Luxation	Ateliotic Pituitary Dwarf	Agility Jog - OK Performing Tricks Tracking Watch Dog	Can be Dog Aggressive, esp. males Alert, spirited, good jumpers; likes to dig, likes to travel Excellent hearing and eyesight
Basenji	**Group:** Hound **Purpose:** Hunter Wild game Sight-hound	22-24 lbs. 16-17 inch	+++ ***	Hip Dysplasia	Ateliotic Pituitary Dwarf	Agility Hunting Jog - Great Lure Coursing Pointing Racing Retrieving Tracking Watch Dog	"Voiceless or Bark-less Dog" Can be Dog Aggressive Do not trust w/ non-canine pets Clean, no doggy odor demanding, active, willful, independent, good climber; needs early socialization Prone to howl or yodel Bred to hunt wild game in Africa. Closely related to the Dingo. They only come into heat once a year
Beagle	**Group:** Hound **Purpose:** Hunter: Rabbits Pheasant Quail Scent - hound	20-30 lbs. 13-15 inch 13 and 15 inch	+++ **	Elbow Dysplasia Hip Dysplasia Patella Luxation	Ateliotic Pituitary Dwarf	Agility Hunting Jog - Good Narcotic Detection Tracking Watch Dog	Do not trust with non-canine pets Lively, sweet curious, willful, excitable, even tempered, not good alone Works well in packs Likes to bay

Small Breed	Group Purpose for breeding	Size Lbs. Ht./ inch	Activity Level+ ---------- Exercise Needs*	Suggested Orthopedic OFA Tests	Body Type	Sport or Activity	More Information
Bedlington Terrier	**Group:** Terrier **Purpose:** Hunter Ratter Badger Fox Retriever	18-23 lbs. 16-17 inch	++ ***	Patellar Luxation	Ateliotic Pituitary Dwarf	**Agility** Hunting **Jog - Good** 'Swimming' **Watch Dog**	*Do not trust with non-canine pets* Very fast, strong willed, energetic courageous, , aggressive, fighter, high strung, difficult to housebreak, likes to dig, loves to chase *Good water dog*
Bichon Frise'	**Group:** Non-sporting **Purpose:** Companion	10-18 lbs. 9-12 inch	++ **	Hip Dysplasia Legg-Calve-Perthes Patella Luxation	Ateliotic Pituitary Dwarf	**Agility** Jog - OK **Obedience Training** Performing Tricks 'Swimming' Watch Dog	'Curly lap dog' Feisty, playful, cheerful, bold, easy to live with, difficult to housebreak, merry *Although not considered a water dog, most do like the water and retrieving*
Border Terrier	**Group:** Terrier **Purpose:** Hunter Fox Vermin	13-19 lbs. 10-12 inch	++ **	Hip Dysplasia Patella Luxation	Ateliotic Pituitary Dwarf	**Agility** Earth Dog **Guide Dog for Blind** Jog - Good **Obedience Training** Performing Tricks **Therapy Dog** Tracking **Watch Dog**	*Do not trust with non-canine pets* Lively, mild mannered, like to run and dig, somewhat confrontational, even tempered, stubborn, can be aggressive, can jump fairly high
Boston Terrier	**Group:** Non-Sporting **Purpose:** Companion	15-25 lbs. 15-17 inch	++ **	Patella Luxation	Ateliotic Pituitary Dwarf Brachycephalic	Jog - OK Watch Dog	"American Gentleman" Expressive, clean, rambunctious; temperaments can vary; gentle, alert, well-mannered, can be stubborn *First non-sporting dog bred in the US* *Do not over exercise in hot/humid weather*

Small   **Dog Breed Chart**

Small Breed	Group Purpose for breeding	Size Lbs. Ht./inch	Activity Level+ ---------- Exercise Needs*	Suggested Orthopedic OFA Tests	Body Types	Sport or Activity	More Information
Bull Terrier (Miniature)	*Group:* Terrier *Purpose:* Companion	20-34 lbs. 10-14 inch	++ **	N/A	Ateliotic Pituitary Dwarf Endomorphic	Jog - OK Obedience Training Performing Tricks Watch Dog	*Can be Dog Aggressive* *Do not trust with non-canine pets* cheerful, fearless, 'clown', strong, willful, fearless, stubborn, courageous *Will not back down to larger dogs*
Cairn Terrier	*Group:* Terrier *Purpose:* Companion Hunter Ratter	14-18 lbs. 10-13 inch	++ **	Patella Luxation	Ateliotic Pituitary Dwarf	Earth Dog Jog - OK Obedience Training Performing Tricks Tracking Watch Dog	Restless, loyal, merry, likes to dig, curious, fearless, sensitive, stubborn, independent *Allergic to fleas* *Left paw dominant*
Cavalier King Charles Spaniel	*Group:* Toy *Purpose:* Companion	13-18 lbs. 12-13 inch	++ **	Hip Dysplasia Patella Luxation	Ateliotic Pituitary Dwarf Brachycephalic	Jog - OK Obedience Training	Sweet. well behaved, patient, eager to please, trusting, adaptable, highly affectionate, some like to perch in high places *Poor sense of direction*
Chinese Crested	*Group:* Toy *Purpose:* Companion *Hairless/Powderpuff*	10 lbs. 9-13 inch	++ **	Elbow Dysplasia Hip Dysplasia Legg-Calve-Perthes	Ateliotic Pituitary Dwarf	Agility Jog - OK Performing Tricks	Sweet. likes to climb and dig, no doggy odor, cuddly, very loving, entertaining, energetic *Comes in both hairless and medium hair. Each have basically the same temperament, but require different grooming techniques*
Cocker Spaniel (American)	*Group:* Sporting *Purpose:* Hunter Bird	18-28 lbs. 14-15 inch	++ **	Hip Dysplasia	Ateliotic Pituitary Dwarf	Agility Hunting Jog - Good Retrieving Tracking Watch Dog	Merry, gentle, trusting, devoted, great with kids, respects authority *Field types generally have a shorter coat and better hunting instincts that show dogs*

Small Breed	Group / Purpose for breeding	Size Lbs. / Ht./ inch	Activity Level+ ----------- Exercise Needs*	Suggested Orthopedic OFA Tests	Body Types	Sport or Activity	More Information
Dachshund	**Group:** Hound **Purpose:** Hunter Badger Rabbit	16-32 lbs. 5-9 inch Mini < 11 lbs.	++ **	Patella Luxation	Ateliotic Pituitary Dwarf Micromelic Achondroplasia	Earth Dog Hunting - Above and below ground Jog - No/OK Performing Tricks Tracking Watch Dog	Good traveler, likes to dig, willful, curious, mischievous, clownish, devoted, likes to chase, stubborn, wary of strangers, clever, loyal Comes in Wire Hair, Short Hair and Long Hair. Wirehaired version may be more clownish, while long haired calmer
Dandie Dinmont Terrier	**Group:** Terrier **Purpose:** Hunter Ratter Rabbit Badger	18-24 lbs. 8-11 inch	+++ **	N/A	Ateliotic Pituitary Dwarf Micromelic Achondroplasia	Hunting Jog - No/OK Tracking Watch Dog	Can be Dog Aggressive. Do not trust with non-canine pets Lively, willful, fun-loving, bold, dignified
English Toy Spaniel AKA*King Charles Spaniel*	**Group:** Toy **Purpose:** Companion	8-14 lbs. 9-10 inch	++ **	Patella Luxation	Ateliotic Pituitary Dwarf Brachycephalic	Jog - OK Watch Dog	Timid, loving, playful, quiet, well-behaved, willful, sweet, not demanding, reserved with strangers Renamed the English Toy Spaniel in North America so it would not be confused with the Cavalier King Charles Spaniel
Finnish Spitz	**Group:** Non-Sporting **Purpose:** Hunter Bird Squirrel Grouse	23-29 lbs. 15- 20 inch	++ **	No Information Available	Ateliotic Pituitary Dwarf	Agility Guard Dog Hunting Jog - Great Obedience Training Tracking Watch Dog	'Barking bird dog' Can be Dog Aggressive Independent, protective, brave, friendly, reserved with strangers, demands attention, hardy dog, loves children Used as a 'bark pointer' mainly for game that goes into trees, but also used for game such as moose and elk
Fox Terrier, Smooth	**Group:** Terrier **Purpose:** Hunter Fox Ratter	15-19 lbs. 12-16 inch	++ **	Legg-Calve-Perthes Patellar Luxation	Ateliotic Pituitary Dwarf	Agility Hunting Jog - OK Performing Tricks Watch Dog	Can be Dog Aggressive. Do not trust with non-canine pets Dominant, energetic, aggressive, independent, protective, bold, loyal Bred for 'fox bolting' & would accompany a pack of foxhounds running after foxes. Well developed hunting skills

Small Breed	Group Purpose for breeding	Size Lbs. ---- Ht./ inch	Activity Level+ ---------- Exercise Needs*	Suggested Orthopedic OFA Tests	Body Types	Sport or Activity	More Information
Fox Terrier, Wire	*Group:* Terrier *Purpose:* Hunter Ratter Fox	15-19 lbs. 12-16 inch	++ **	Patella Luxation	Ateliotic Pituitary Dwarf	Agility Hunting Jog - OK Performing Tricks Watch Dog	*Can be Dog Aggressive.* *Do not trust with non-canine pets* Dominant, energetic, aggressive, independent, protective, loyal *Bred to chase foxes into their burrows underground, and their short tails were used as handles by the hunter to pull them back out.* *Better with children than Smooth Fox*
French Bulldog	*Group:* Non-Sporting *Purpose:* Hunter Ratter Companion	28 lbs. 12 inch	++ **	Elbow Dysplasia Hip Dysplasia Patella Luxation	Ateliotic Pituitary Dwarf Brachycephalic	Jog - No Therapy Dog Watch Dog	Sweet, playful, easygoing, willful, can be snappish, reserved with strangers, curious, alert, devoted, good w/ kids/pets when raised together *Difficult to breed usually requiring cesarean section* *Do not exercise in hot/humid weather*
Havanese	*Group:* Toy *Purpose:* Companion	8-14 lbs. 8-11 inch	++ **	Hip Dysplasia Patellar Luxation	Ateliotic Pituitary Dwarf	Agility Flyball Jog - OK Mold/Termite Detection Obedience Training Performing Tricks Therapy Dog Tracking Watch Dog	Charming, smart, loves people, needy, energetic, sociable, good with kids and other animals, very curious *Good at Musical canine freestyle* *Hair can be corded*
Irish Terrier	*Group:* Terrier *Purpose:* Hunter Ratter Otter Vermin Retriever	25-27 lbs. 18 inch	++ **	Hip Dysplasia	Ateliotic Pituitary Dwarf	Agility Guard Dog Hunting Jog - Good Retrieving Tracking Watch Dog	*Can be Dog Aggressive* *Do not trust with non-canine pets* Likes to dig and chase, reckless, fearless, courageous, spirited, loyal, plays hard, protective, affectionate *Has also been used as a wartime messenger*

Small Breed	Group Purpose for breeding	Size Lbs. Ht./inch	Activity Level+ ----------- Exercise Needs*	Suggested Orthopedic OFA Tests	Body Types	Sport or Activity	More Information
Lakeland Terrier	**Group:** Terrier **Purpose:** Hunter Fox Rabbit Vermin	17 lbs. 13-15 inch	+++ **	No Information Available	Ateliotic Pituitary Dwarf	Hunting Jog - Good/Great Tracking Watch Dog	*Dog Aggressive* *Do not trust with non-canine pets* Friendly, bold, confident, feisty, likes to dig, difficult to housebreak, alert, willful, courageous, independent *Bred to kill foxes in their den*
Lhasa Apso	**Group:** Non-Sporting **Purpose:** Watchdog Companion	16 lbs. 9-11 inch	+++ **	No Information Available	Ateliotic Pituitary Dwarf Brachycephalic	Jog - OK Watch Dog	*Not good with non-canine pets* Devoted, lively, good hearing, travels well, energetic, fearless, does not like the water *Like to burrow into 'caves' and perch up in high places* *Bred as an indoor monastery sentinel dog by Tibetan Buddhist monks*
Lowchen	**Group:** Non-Sporting **Purpose:** Watchdog Companion	12-18 lbs. 12-14 inch	++ **	Hip Dysplasia Patellar Luxation	Ateliotic Pituitary Dwarf	Agility Jog - OK Obedience Training Performing Tricks Watch Dog	*'Little Lion Dog'* Cheerful, curious, affectionate, likes to cuddle, travels well, friendly, happy, very intelligent *Used by the 'ladies' of the castle as a sort of 'living hot water bottle'*
Manchester Terrier (Standard) **AKA Rat Terrier**	**Group:** Terrier **Purpose:** Hunter Ratter	12-22 lbs. 17 inch	+++ **	Legg-Calve-Perthes Patella Luxation	Ateliotic Pituitary Dwarf	Agility Jog - Good Watch Dog	*Not good with non-canine pets* Headstrong, protective, active, likes to run, willful, headstrong, high prey drive *Used in England in the early 1800s in the 'sport' of rat killing and rabbit coursing*
Miniature Schnauzer	**Group:** Terrier **Purpose:** Hunter Ratter	13-19 lbs. 12-14 inch	+++ ***	N/A	Ateliotic Pituitary Dwarf	Agility Guard Dog Jog - Good Performing Tricks Tracking Watch Dog	*Can be Dog Aggressive* Alert, spirited, obedient to command, willing to please, protective, territorial, high prey drive, can be dominant *Dry ears' after swimming to reduce risk of infection*

Small Breed	Group **Purpose for breeding**	Size Lbs. Ht./inch	Activity Level+ ---------- Exercise Needs*	Suggested Orthopedic OFA Tests	Body Types	Sport or Activity	More Information
  Parsons Russell Terrier	*Group:* Terrier *Purpose:* Hunter Fox	13-17 lbs. 12-14 inch	+++ ***	Patellar Luxation	**Ateliotic Pituitary Dwarf**	**Agility** Earth Dog **Hunting** Jog - Good **Obedience Training** Performing Tricks **Service Dog** Tracking **Watch Dog**	*Can be Dog Aggressive* *Not good with non-canine pets* *Easily bored, perky, fearless, clever, determined, needs to keep entertained*
  Poodle (Miniature)	*Group:* Non-Sporting *Purpose:* Hunter Bird Retriever	15-17 lbs. 11-15 inch	+++ **	Hip Dysplasia Patellar Luxation	**Ateliotic Pituitary Dwarf**	**Agility** Hunting Jog - OK Obedience Training **Performing Tricks** Retrieving **Tracking** Watch Dog	*Extremely intelligent, trainable, pleasant, happy, clever, reserved with strangers, can 'understand speech', can be high strung* *Bred as a water dog – good at many water sports* *One of the most intelligent and trainable breeds* *Some state that the show clip is actually a working clip where the joints are covered to protect from the cold water, some skeptics asked why other breeds do not need this same clip. The clip may have possibly come from their days as circus performers*

Small Breed	Group Purpose for breeding	Size Lbs. ___ Ht./ inch	Activity Level+ ---------- Exercise Needs*	Suggested Orthopedic OFA Tests	Body Types	Sport or Activity	More Information
Pyrenean Shepherd	*Group:* Herding *Purpose:* Herder Sheep	30-55 lbs. 15- 21 inch	++ ***	Hip Dysplasia Patella Luxation	Ateliotic Pituitary Dwarf	Agility Disc Dog Flyball Herding Jog - Good Obedience Training Performing Tricks Search & Rescue Service Dog Tracking Watch Dog	*Can be Dog Aggressive* Good with children/pets when raised together, very wary of strangers, playful, alert, loyal, intelligent, mischievous *Comes in two coats : smooth and rough (semi-long or long-haired)*
Pug	*Group:* Toy *Purpose:* Companion	14-18 lbs. 10-11 inch	++ **	Elbow Dysplasia Hip Dysplasia Patella Luxation	Ateliotic Pituitary Dwarf Brachycephalic	Jog - No Obedience Training Performing Tricks Watch Dog	Sweet, wary of strangers, brave, dignified, willful, possessive, confident, lap dog *Do not overfeed – Prone to obesity* *Bred to adorn the laps of the Chinese sovereigns* *Prone to 'reverse sneeze', snoring and snorting due to shortened snout and elongated palate* *Do not over exercise in hot/humid weather*
Schipperke	*Group:* Non-Sport *Purpose:* Hunter Ratter	18 lbs. 12-13 inch	+++ **	Hip Dysplasia Patella Luxation	Ateliotic Pituitary Dwarf	Agility Guard Dog Herding Jog - Good Obedience Training Performing Tricks Watch Dog	'Belgian Ship Dog' Protective, wary of strangers, curious, energetic, good only if raised with other pets, bored with repetition *Often seen on boats – Not prone to seasickness* *Also bred to nip at towing horses heels to keep them moving*

Small Breed	Group Purpose for breeding	Size Lbs. Ht./ inch	Activity Level+ ----------- Exercise Needs*	Suggested Orthopedic OFA Tests	Body Types	Sport or Activity	More Information
Scottish Terrier	*Group:* Terrier *Purpose:* Hunter Fox Badger Rabbit	18-22 lbs. 10 inch	++ **	Patella Luxation	Ateliotic Pituitary Dwarf Micromelic Achondroplasia	Agility Jog - OK Performing Tricks Watch Dog	Likes to dig, prey driven, protective, quick moving, feisty, challenging, independent, snappish *Do not overfeed* *Keep on leash due to strong prey drive*
Sealyham Terrier	*Group:* Terrier *Purpose:* Hunter Ratter Fox Badgers	23 lbs. 10-12 inch	++ **	N/A	Ateliotic Pituitary Dwarf Micromelic Achondroplasia	Jog - OK Tracking Watch Dog	*Can be Dog Aggressive* Fun loving, good with older adults, brave, not as rowdy as some terriers, good when raised with kids or other animals, even tempered, relaxed, 'couch potato'
Shetland Sheepdog	*Group:* Herding *Purpose:* Herder Sheep	18 lbs. 13-16 inch	++ **	Hip Dysplasia Patella Luxation	Ateliotic Pituitary Dwarf	Agility Flyball Herding Jog - Good Obedience Training Performing Tricks Tracking Watch Dog	Gentle, sensitive, eager to please, lively, very smart, reserved with strangers *May try to 'herd' kids and other pets* **Working Dog:** *Needs to have a job to do to keep mentally and physically stimulated. Gets bored easily*
Shiba Inu	*Group:* Non-Sporting *Purpose:* Hunter Bird	17-23 lbs. 13-16 inch	++ **	Hip Dysplasia Patella Luxation	Ateliotic Pituitary Dwarf	Agility Guard Dog Hunting Jog - Good Performing Tricks Tracking Watch Dog	*Can be Dog Aggressive w/ same sex dogs.* *Don't trust with rodents/birds* Lively, fearless, active, confident, independent, loving *Keep on leash due to strong prey drive* *Extremely clean dogs that wash themselves like a cat* *"Shiba Scream" when provoked or unhappy*
Skye Terrier	*Group:* Terrier *Purpose:* Hunter Ratter Companion	25 lbs. 9-10 inch	++ **	No Information Available	Ateliotic Pituitary Dwarf Micromelic Achondroplasia	Jog - OK Watch Dog	*Can be Dog Aggressive* *Not good with other pets* Sensitive, protective, courageous, serious, prey driven, can be snappish, loving, playful, more serious than other terriers

Small Breed	Group *Purpose for breeding*	<u>Size</u> Lbs. Ht./ inch	Activity Level+ ------------ Exercise Needs*	Suggested Orthopedic OFA Tests	Body Types	Sport or Activity	More Information
Swedish Vallhund	*Group:* Herding *Purpose:* Herder Cattle Hunter Ratter Watch Dog	25-35 lbs. 11.5-13.5 inch	++ ***	Hip Dysplasia	Ateliotic Pituitary Dwarf Micromelic Achondroplasia	**Agility** Herding **Jog - Good/OK** Performing Tricks **Retrieving** Search & Rescue **Tracking** Watch Dog	'Viking Dog' Watchful, energetic, fearless, friendly, loyal, eager to please, fast, powerful, healthy *May try to 'herd' kids and other pets by nipping at feet* ***Working Dog****: Needs to have a job to do to keep mentally and physically stimulated. Gets bored easily*
Tibetan Terrier	*Group:* Non-Sporting *Purpose:* Guard Dog Companion	20-24 lbs. 14-16 inch	++ **	Elbow Dysplasia Hip Dysplasia Patellar Luxation	Ateliotic Pituitary Dwarf	**Agility** Herding **Jog - OK** Obedience Training **Watch Dog**	'Lucky Temple Dog' Gentle, loving, willful, wary of strangers, determined, clever, can be jealous *Not actually a terrier Breed was originally given as gifts in Tibet and were thought to be lucky and too precious to be sold*
Welsh Corgi Cardigan	*Group:* Herding *Purpose:* Herder Sheep Cattle Hunter Ratter	25-38 lbs. 10.5-12.5 inch	+++ ***	Hip Dysplasia	Ateliotic Pituitary Dwarf Micromelic Achondroplasia	**Agility** Guard Dog **Herding** Jog - Good **Tracking** Watch Dog	Can be Dog Aggressive Robust, obedient, protective, loyal, eager to please, wary of strangers *May try to 'herd' kids and other pets by nipping at feet* *Not great swimmers* ***Working Dog****: Needs to have a job to do to keep mentally and physically stimulated. Gets bored easily* *Not as social & can be more territorial than the Pembroke*

Small Breed	Group **Purpose for breeding**	Size Lbs. Ht./inch	Activity Level+ ---------- Exercise Needs*	Suggested Orthopedic OFA Tests	Body Types	Sport or Activity	More Information
Welsh Corgi Pembroke	*Group:* Herding *Purpose:* Herder Sheep Cattle Horses Hunter Ratter	27-30 lbs. 10- 12 inch	+++ ***	Hip Dysplasia	Ateliotic Pituitary Dwarf Micromelic Achondroplasia	Agility Guard Dog Herding Jog - Good Obedience Training Tracking Watch Dog	Hardy, obedient, protective, outgoing, devoted, athletic, reserved with strangers *May try to 'herd' kids and other pets by nipping at feet* *Not great swimmers* ***Working Dog**: Needs to have a job to do to keep mentally and physically stimulated. Gets bored easily*
Welsh Terrier	*Group:* Terrier *Purpose:* Hunter Fox Badgers Ratter	18-20 lbs. 14-15 inch	+++ ***	N/A	Ateliotic Pituitary Dwarf	Agility Jog - Great Performing Tricks Tracking Watch Dog	*Can be Dog Aggressive* Hardy, curious, spunky, active, reserved with strangers, likes to chase, can be dominant *Keep on leash due to a strong prey drive*
West Highland White Terrier	*Group:* Terrier *Purpose:* Hunter Ratter Fox	15-18 lbs. 10-11 inch	+++ **	Hip Dysplasia Patellar Luxation	Ateliotic Pituitary Dwarf	Jog - OK Performing Tricks Watch Dog	*Do not trust w/ non-canine pets.* Lively, self assured, spunky, outgoing, happy, devoted, easy to travel with, likes to chase *Do not over-bath, as prone to skin allergies and dryness*
Whippet	*Group:* Hound *Purpose:* Racing Sight-Hound	10-28 lbs. 18- 22 inch	++ ***	Hip Dysplasia	Ateliotic Pituitary Dwarf Ectomorphic	Agility Flyball Hunting Jog -Great Lure Coursing Racing Watch Dog	*'Poor Man's Racehorse'* *Do not trust w/ non-canine pets.* Affectionate, sweet, quiet, calm, sensitive, can be difficult to housebreak, travels well, couch potato *Can reach 37 MPH in seconds* *Keep on leash, as they do not have good traffic sense*

Medium Breed	Group / Purpose for breeding	Size Lbs. / Ht./ inch	Activity Level+ / Exercise Needs*	Suggested Orthopedic OFA Tests	Body Type	Sport or Activity	More Information
Airedale Terrier	*Group:* Terrier *Purpose:* Hunter Ratter Large Game Guard Dog	45-60 lbs. 21-23 inch	+++ ****	Elbow Dysplasia Hip Dysplasia	Mesomorphic	Agility, Guard Dog, Hunting, Jog - Great, Obedience Training, Schutzhund / Ring Sports, Tracking, Watch Dog	*Can be Dog Aggressive* Playful, patient, protective, spirited, eager to please, responsive, strong willed, good swimmer, stoic, independent, fearless, high tolerance to pain. *Working Dog:* Needs to have a job to do to keep mentally and physically stimulated. Gets bored easily
American Pitt Bull Terrier	*Group:* Terrier *Purpose:* Bull Baiting Guard Dog	30-60 lbs. 16-20 inch	+++ ****	Elbow Dysplasia Hip Dysplasia	Endomorphic	Carting, Guard Dog, Jog - Good, Obedience Training, Performing Tricks, Schutzhund / Ring Sports, Therapy Dog, Tracking, Watch Dog, Weight Pulling	*Can be Dog Aggressive, esp. same sex dogs. Do not trust w/ non-canine pets* Likes to dig, athletic, likes to jump and climb, high pain tolerance, alert, outgoing, courageous, willful, impulsive, devoted, strong prey drive. *Great family dog if raised properly and purchased from a reputable breeder*
American Staffordshire Terrier	*Group:* Terrier *Purpose:* Bull Baiting Hunter Pig Bear Guard Dog	40-70 lbs. 17-19 inch	+++ ****	Elbow Dysplasia Hip Dysplasia	Endomorphic	Carting, Guard Dog, Jog - Good, Obedience Training, Schutzhund / Ring Sports, Therapy Dog, Watch Dog, Weight Pulling	*Can be Dog Aggressive, esp. same sex dogs. Do not trust w/ non-canine pets* Likes to dig, athletic, likes to jump and climb, high pain tolerance, courageous, willful, impulsive, devoted, strong prey drive. *Originally bred to 'bait' bears or bulls'. Great family dog if raised properly and purchased from a reputable breeder*

Medium Breed	Group *Purpose for breeding*	<u>Size</u> Lbs. Ht./ inch	Activity Level+ ---------- Exercise Needs*	Suggested Orthopedic OFA Tests	Body Type	Sport or Activity	More Information
 American Water Spaniel	*Group:* Sporting *Purpose:* Hunter Bird Retriever	25-45 lbs. 15-18 inch	++ **	Hip Dysplasia	Mesomorphic	**Agility** Canicross **Dock Diving** Guard Dog **Hunting** Jog - Great **Obedience Training** Retrieving **Tracking** Watch Dog	Eager, enjoys working, friendly, excellent swimmer, protective of owner, willing to please, can be temperamental, likes to roam *Used for flushing and retrieving game (land and water)* *Soft mouthed*
 Australian Cattle Dog **AKA Queensland Heeler, Blue Heeler**	*Group:* Herding *Purpose:* Herder Cattle	25-45 lbs. 15-18 inch	++ ****	Elbow Dysplasia Hip Dysplasia Patella Luxation	Mesomorphic	**Agility** Bikejoring **Canicross** Guard Dog **Herding** Jog - Great **Obedience Training** Performing Tricks **Retrieving** Watch Dog	*Can be Dog Aggressive, esp. same sex dogs. Do not trust w/ non-canine pets* Protective, alert, active, intelligent, brave, independent, cautious towards strangers *May try to 'herd' kids and other pets by nipping at feet* *Working Dog: Needs to have a job to do to keep mentally and physically stimulated. Gets bored easily*

Medium Breed	Group Purpose for breeding	Size Lbs. Ht./inch	Activity Level+ ---------- Exercise Needs*	Suggested Orthopedic OFA Tests	Body Type	Sport or Activity	More Information
  Australian Shepherd	*Group:* Herding *Purpose:* Herder Cattle Sheep	30-55 lbs. 18- 23 inch	+++ ****	Elbow Dysplasia Hip Dysplasia	Mesomorphic	Agility Bikejoring Canicross Disc Dog Flyball Herding Jog - Great Narcotic Detection Obedience Training Performing Tricks Retrieving Search & Rescue Service Dog Watch Dog	Easy going, protective, agile, lively, attentive, gentle, quick learner, intelligent, very loyal *Used for herding unusual livestock as well, such as ducks and rabbits* ***Working Dog***: *Needs to have a job to do to keep mentally and physically stimulated. Gets bored easily*
  Basset Hound	*Group:* Hound *Purpose:* Scent -Hound	55-65 lbs. 13-15 inch	+ ***	N/A	Micromelic Achondroplasia	Hunting Jog - No/OK Performing Tricks Tracking Watch Dog	Gentle, devoted, peaceful, sweet natured *Not good swimmers* ***Motivated by their nose in training, so use treats*** ***Howl to warn of danger or when scared. Low murmur or whine when they want something***
  Bearded Collie	*Group:* Herding *Purpose:* Herder Sheep Cattle	35-60 lbs. 20- 22 inch	++ ****	Hip Dysplasia	Mesomorphic	Agility Canicross Herding Jog - Great Obedience Training Performing Tricks Tracking Watch Dog	Very energetic, bouncy, happy-go-lucky, stable, enthusiastic, can be headstrong ***Working Dog***: *Needs to have a job to do to keep mentally and physically stimulated. Gets bored easily*

Medium Breed	Group Purpose for breeding	Size Lbs. Ht./inch	Activity Level+ --------- Exercise Needs*	Suggested Orthopedic OFA Tests	Body Type	Sport or Activity	More Information
Border Collie	**Group:** Herding **Purpose:** Herder Cattle Sheep Livestock	30-60 lbs. 18- 22 inch	+++ ****	Elbow Dysplasia Hip Dysplasia	Mesomorphic	Agility Bikejoring Canicross Disc Dog Flyball Herding Jog - Great Narcotic Detection Obedience Training Performing Tricks Retrieving Search & Rescue Skijoring Therapy Dog Watch Dog	*Can be Dog Aggressive, esp. same sex dogs* *Do not trust w/ non-canine pets* Good concentration level, easily bored, can be dominating, sensitive hearing *The herding breed & show/companion breeds have differences in their personalities. If you are looking for a companion, do not buy collies that were bred for herding and vice versa* *Working Dog: Needs to have a job to do to keep mentally and physically stimulated. Gets bored easily* *Excels at most 'sports'*
Brittany	**Group:** Sporting **Purpose:** Hunter Bird Retriever Pointer	30-40 lbs. 17.5-21.5 inch	+++ ****	Elbow Dysplasia Hip Dysplasia	Mesomorphic	Agility Canicross Jog - Great Pointing Retrieving	Likes to roam, gentle, active, independent, happy, alert, can be willful; can be shy if not well socialized *Working Dog: Needs to have a job to do to keep mentally and physically stimulated. Gets bored easily*
Bulldog (English)	**Group:** Non-Sporting **Purpose:** Bull baiting Bear baiting	40-50 lbs. 14-17 inch	+ **	Elbow Dysplasia Hip Dysplasia Patella Luxation	Endomorphic	Jog - No/OK Obedience Training Watch Dog Weight Pulling	*Can be Dog Aggressive,* Gentle, devoted, eager to please, protective of family *Cannot swim – use dog water vest if near water* *Needs to be walked, but not intense exercise* *Difficult to breed usually requiring cesarean section*

Medium Breed	Group Purpose for breeding	Size Lbs. Ht./ inch	Activity Level+ ---------- Exercise Needs*	Suggested Orthopedic OFA Tests	Body Type	Sport or Activity	More Information
Bull Terrier	*Group:* Terrier *Purpose:* Guard Dog	35-80 lbs. 15-22 inch	++ **	Patella Luxation	Endomorphic	Agility Canicross Jog - Great Obedience Training Performing Tricks Watch Dog Weight Pulling	*Can be Dog Aggressive, esp. same sex dogs Do not trust w/ non-canine pets* Cheerful, fearless, greedy, 'clown', strong, willful, fearless *Can become destructive if not well socialized and entertained*
Canaan Dog	*Group:* Herding *Purpose:* Herder Sheep Guard Dog	35-55 lbs. 19- 24 inch	++ ***	Elbow Dysplasia Hip Dysplasia Patella Luxation	Mesomorphic	Agility Bikejoring Canicross Guard Dog Herding Jog - Great Narcotic Detection Obedience Training Skijoring Tracking Watch Dog	Becomes bored with repetitive training, devoted, docile, no doggy odor, lively, protective, healthy dog, strong survival instincts, quick learners, defensive of territory/family, good w/ kids/pets if raised together *Working Dog:* Needs to have a job to do to keep mentally and physically stimulated. Gets bored easily
Chinese Shar-Pei	*Group:* Non-Sporting *Purpose:* Guard Dog Hunter Pigs Herder Cattle	40-60 lbs. 18-20 inch	++ **	Elbow Dysplasia Hip Dysplasia Patella Luxation	Mesomorphic	Agility Herding Hunting Jog - Good Performing Tricks Watch Dog	*Can be Dog Aggressive* Very clean, does not like water, devoted, protective, reserved w/ strangers, willful, regal, aloof, calm, confident, can be territorial ** 3 types of coats: Brush, bear and horse (very rough). **The different coats on these breeds can depict different personalities – talk to breeders for more info*** *Originally bred as palace guards in China* *Can be allergic to food products that contain soy, corn, wheat, glutens & sugars*

Medium Breed	Group Purpose for breeding	Size Lbs. Ht./inch	Activity Level+ ---------- Exercise Needs*	Suggested Orthopedic OFA Tests	Body Type	Sport or Activity	More Information
Clumber Spaniel	Group: Sporting Purpose: Hunter Bird	55-85 lbs. 17-20 inch	+ ***	Elbow Dysplasia Hip Dysplasia	Micromelic Achondroplasia	Hunting Tracking Retrieving Jog - Good	Good stamina, reserved w/ strangers, good swimmer, likes to fetch, needs chew toys, likes to walk, gentle, well behaved, quiet, playful, loyal, *Drools, wheezes, snores* *Good at upland hunting in heavy cover* *Discourage jumping due to poor hips*
Chow Chow	Group: Non-Sporting Purpose: Sled Dog Hunter birds > wolves	70 lbs. 20 inch	++ **	Elbow Dysplasia Hip Dysplasia Patella Luxation	Mesomorphic	Carting Guard Dog Herding Jog - Good Sledding Watch Dog	'Puffy lion dog' *Can be Dog Aggressive* Bossy, serious, independent, reserved, dominant, very protective, willful, gets bored with repetition, natural problem solver, very reserved w/ strangers *Working Dog:* Needs to have a job to do to keep mentally and physically stimulated
Dalmation	Group: Non-Sporting Purpose: Guard Dog Hunter Ratter Bird Boar Retriever	40-70 lbs. 19-24 inch	+++ ****	Hip Dysplasia	Mesomorphic	Agility Bikejoring Canicross Disc Dog Flyball Herding Hunting Jog - Great Obedience Training Performing Tricks Retrieving Search & Rescue Tracking Watch Dog	*Can be Dog Aggressive* No doggy odor, hardy, energetic, playful, high strung, willful, fast, good stamina, good memory, good survival instincts, protective *Originally bred as a carriage dog running aside the coach, and then guarding it when unoccupied* *Used to guard the firehouse* *Hunts well in packs* *Buy from reputable breeder that has checked for congenital deafness in puppies*

Medium Breed	Group / Purpose for breeding	Size Lbs. / Ht./ inch	Activity Level+ ----------- Exercise Needs*	Suggested Orthopedic OFA Tests	Body Type	Sport or Activity	More Information
English Cocker Spaniel	**Group:** Sporting **Purpose:** Hunter Bird Retriever	27-34 lbs. 15-17 inch	++ ***	Hip Dysplasia Patella Luxation	Mesomorphic	Agility Hunting Jog - Good Retrieving Tracking Watch Dog	*Do not trust w/ non-canine pets* Merry, gentle, trusting, devoted, great with kids, respects authority, can be stubborn *Do not overfeed* *The working breed & show/companion breeds have differences in their personalities. If you are looking for a companion, do not buy spaniels that were bred as hunting dogs and vice versa* *'Soft mouthed'* *Although rare, "Rage Syndrome' has been seen in this breed where the dog will unexplainably attack. Found more in solid color/show breeds*
English Springer Spaniel	**Group:** Sporting **Purpose:** Hunter Bird Retriever	44-55 lbs. 19-20 inch	++ ***	Elbow Dysplasia Hip Dysplasia	Mesomorphic	Agility Canicross Hunting Jog - Great Obedience Training Retrieving Tracking Watch Dog	Playful, gentle, brave, sweet, energetic, quick to learn, willing to obey, great stamina, alert *Do not overfeed* **As this dog is bred to hunt birds, it is not a good idea to have birds as other pets** *Although rare, "Rage Syndrome' has been seen in this breed where the dog will unexplainably attack*
Field Spaniel	**Group:** Sporting **Purpose:** Hunter Bird Retriever	35-50 lbs. 16-19 inch	++ ***	Elbow Dysplasia Hip Dysplasia Patella Luxation	Mesomorphic	Agility Canicross Hunting Jog - Great Retrieving Tracking Watch Dog	Playful, mild mannered, sweet, active, good with kids, vigorous, likes to roam *Do not overfeed* **As this dog is bred to hunt birds, it is not a good idea to have birds as other pets** **Rare in the US**

Medium Breed	Group / Purpose for breeding	Size Lbs. / Ht./ inch	Activity Level+ ---------- Exercise Needs*	Suggested Orthopedic OFA Tests	Body Type	Sport or Activity	More Information
German Pinscher	**Group:** Working **Purpose:** Hunter Ratter Guard Dog	25-45 lbs. 17-20 inch	++ ****	Hip Dysplasia	Mesomorphic	Agility Canicross Guard Dog Jog - Great Obedience Training Performing Tricks Search & Rescue Therapy Dog Tracking Watch Dog	*Can be Dog Aggressive* Fearless, very protective, territorial, possessive of items, strong willed, stubborn, dominant, quick learner, loving, likes to be with you, high prey drive *Temperament is hereditary, so choose carefully when picking a pup* *Working Dog: Needs to have a job to do to keep mentally and physically stimulated* *Does not do well with repetitive training*
Glen of Imaal Terrier	**Group:** Terrier **Purpose:** Hunter Ratter Fox Badger	30-40 lbs. 12-14 inch	++ **	Elbow Dysplasia Hip Dysplasia	Micromelic Achondroplasia	Agility Earth Dog Guard Dog Hunting Jog - No/OK Watch Dog	*Can be Dog Aggressive, esp. same sex dogs Do not trust w/ non-canine pets* Tough, spirited, cocky, brave, patient, loyal, playful, active, reserved with strangers, strong prey drive
Harrier	**Group:** Hound **Purpose:** Hunter Rabbit Fox Pack Dog	40-55 lbs. 19-21 inch	++ ***	Hip Dysplasia	Mesomorphic	Agility Canicross Hunting Jog - Great Obedience Training Tracking Watch Dog	*Do not trust w/ non-canine pets* Active, merry, sweet tempered, likes to explore *Bays instead of barks* *Needs to be part of a pack, whether other dogs or humans* *Working Dog: Needs to have a job to do to keep mentally and physically stimulated*

Medium Breed	Group / Purpose for breeding	Size Lbs. / Ht./ inch	Activity Level+ ---------- Exercise Needs*	Suggested Orthopedic OFA Tests	Body Type	Sport or Activity	More Information
Ibizan Hound	**Group:** Hound **Purpose:** Scent - Hound Sight -Hound Pointer Retriever	45-50 lbs. 22-26 inch	++ ***	Hip Dysplasia	Ectomorphic	Agility Hunting Jog - Great Lure Coursing Pointing Racing Retrieving Tracking	*Can be Dog Aggressive, esp. same sex dogs. Do not trust w/ non-canine pets* Quiet, clean, polite, willful, gets bored easily, protective, can jump high, likes to run *Also comes in a wire hair or long hair version* *Escape artists to due ability to climb and jump very high* *Hunt in packs of almost all females. Can hunt on most terrain by sight, sound and smell*
Irish Water Spaniel	**Group:** Sporting **Purpose:** Hunter Bird Retriever	45-65 lbs. 21- 24 inch	++ ***	Elbow Dysplasia Hip Dysplasia	Mesomorphic	Agility Canicross Dock Diving Hunting Jog - Great Obedience Training Retrieving Tracking Watch Dog	Loves swimming, eager to please, bold, confident, devoted, mischievous, reserved with strangers *Working Dog: Needs to have a job to do to keep mentally and physically stimulated*
Keeshond	**Group:** Non-Sporting **Purpose:** Guard Dog	35-40 lbs. 17-18 inch	++ ***	Elbow Dysplasia Hip Dysplasia Patellar Luxation	Mesomorphic	Agility Guard Dog Jog - Good Performing Tricks Watch Dog	Lively, intelligent, outgoing, friendly, good jumper, quick reflexes, quick learners, intuitive, can be clingy with their owners (Velcro dog) *Needs people; not a good dog for someone who plans to be away or keep them in a kennel or yard* *Named after a leader of the Dutch rebellion and later used as guard dogs on barges*

Medium Breed	Group / Purpose for breeding	Size Lbs. / Ht./ inch	Activity Level+ ---------- Exercise Needs*	Suggested Orthopedic OFA Tests	Body Type	Sport or Activity	More Information

Kerry Blue Terrier	*Group:* Terrier
	
	Purpose: Hunter
	  Rabbits
	  Badger
	
	Retriever
	
	Herder
	  Sheep
	  Cattle
	
	Guard Dog
		33-40 lbs.
		
		17-19.5 inch
			++
			
			***
				Hip Dysplasia	Mesomorphic	Agility
						
						Guard Dog
						
						Herding
						
						Hunting
						
						Jog - Good
						
						Obedience Training
						
						Retrieving
						
						Tracking
						
						Watch Dog
							Can be Dog Aggressive Spirited, boisterous, playful, likes roughhousing, willful, determined, friendly, strong-headed, loyal, affectionate, fast
							
							National dog of Ireland

Norwegian Buhund	*Group:* Herding
	
	Purpose: Watch
	  Dog
	
	Hunter
	  Ratter
	  Squirrel
	  Bear
	  Wolves
	
	Herder
		48-55 lbs.
		
		16-19 inch
			++
			
			***
				Hip Dysplasia	Mesomorphic	Agility
						
						Assistant - Deaf
						
						Flyball
						
						Herding
						
						Hunting
						
						Jog - Good
						
						Narcotic Detection
						
						Obedience Training
						
						Tracking
						
						Watch Dog
							Cheerful, friendly, active, athletic, gets bored easily, eager to please, headstrong, alert, agile, quick learner
							
							Working Dog: Needs to have a job to do to keep mentally and physically stimulated
							
							This breed has been found in many Viking burial grounds

Norwegian Elkhound	*Group:* Hound
	
	Purpose: Hunter
	  Moose
	  Bear
	  Wolves
		26-40 lbs.
		
		19-20.5 inch
			++
			
			***
				Hip Dysplasia
				Patellar Luxation
					Mesomorphic	Agility
						
						Bikejoring
						
						Canicross
						
						Guard Dog
						
						Herding
						
						Hunting
						
						Jog - Great
						
						Skijoring
						
						Sledding / Mushing
						
						Tracking
						
						Watch Dog
							Can be Dog Aggressive, esp. same sex dogs. Do not trust w/ non-canine pets Loyal to their 'pack', alert independent, fearless, energetic, clean, docile, boisterous protective, no doggy odor, can be dominant
							
							Do not overfeed
							
							A true outside dog, but does not do well in the heat

Medium Breed	Group Purpose for breeding	Size Lbs. Ht./ inch	Activity Level+ ----------- Exercise Needs*	Suggested Orthopedic OFA Tests	Body Type	Sport or Activity	More Information
Nova Scotia Duck Tolling Retriever	*Group:* Sporting *Purpose:* Hunter Bird Retriever	37-51 lbs. 17-21 inch	++ ****	Hip Dysplasia	Mesomorphic	**Agility** Dock Diving **Hunting** Jog - Great **Obedience Training** Performing Tricks **Retrieving** Search & Rescue **Therapy Dog** Tracking **Watch Dog**	Reserved with strangers, determined, alert, gentle, great swimmer, prey driven, outgoing, ready for action, patient *Working Dog: Needs to have a job to do to keep mentally and physically stimulated* *Official dog of Nova Scotia*
Petit Basset Griffon Vendeen (PBGV)	*Group:* Hound *Purpose:* Hunter Rabbit	30-38 lbs. 13-15 inch	++ **	No Information Available	Micromelic Achondroplasia	**Agility** Hunting **Jog - OK** Obedience Training **Therapy Dog** Tracking	*Do not trust w/ non-canine pets* Merry, friendly, loves to explore, willful, curious, confident, likes to dig and jump, extroverted, escape artists, stubborn, extroverted, prey driven *Can hunt in packs & Likes to howl*
Pharaoh Hound	*Group:* Hound *Purpose:* Hunter Rabbit Bird Sight - Hound	45-60 lbs. 21-25 inch	++ ****	Hip Dysplasia Patellar Luxation	Ectomorphic	**Agility** Canicross **Hunting** Jog - Great **Lure Coursing** Obedience Training **Racing** Tracking **Watch Dog**	*Do not trust w/ non-canine pets* Reserved with strangers, loves to play, calm, loving, fast, clean w/ no doggy odor, gets bored easily w/ repetitive commands, active, can be stubborn, strong prey drive, good at jumping *'Blushes' when they get excited w/ ears & nose getting pink* *National dog of Malta*

Medium Breed	Group **Purpose for breeding**	Size Lbs. Ht./inch	Activity Level+ ---------- Exercise Needs*	Suggested Orthopedic OFA Tests	Body Type	Sport or Activity	More Information
Plott Hound	*Group:* Hound *Purpose:* Hunter Boar Bear Scent - Hound	40-60 lbs. 20-25 inch	++ ***	No Information Available	Mesomorphic	**Guard Dog** Hunting **Jog - OK** Tracking **Watch Dog**	Smart, loyal, alert, eager to please, active, fast, bright, confident, courageous, great stamina *Some lines are not good with other animals, and can be aggressive, as they were bred to hunt/fight large game, such as boar, large cats and bear*
Polish Lowland Sheepdog *AKA* Polish Owczarek Nizinny or PON	*Group:* Herding *Purpose:* Herder Sheep	35-40 lbs. 17- 20 inch	++ **	Hip Dysplasia	Micromelic Achondroplasia	**Agility** Herding **Jog - OK** Obedience Training **Performing Tricks** Watch Dog	Alert, eager to please, clownish, great memory, stubborn, intelligent, wary of strangers, adapts well, can be dominant *May try to 'herd' kids and other pets* 'Kleptomaniacs' *Working Dog: Needs to have a job to do to keep mentally and physically stimulated*
Portuguese Water Dog	*Group:* Working *Purpose:* Retriever Water	35-60 lbs. 17- 23 inch	++ ***	Hip Dysplasia Patella Luxation	Mesomorphic	**Agility** Canicross **Guard Dog** Jog - Great **Obedience Training** Retrieving **Therapy Dog** Watch Dog **Water Rescue**	Excellent swimmer, reserved w/ strangers, lively, sensible, pleasant, stable, eager to please, good stamina *Bred to herd fish into fishermen's nets, retrieve lost tackle or broken nets, and to act as couriers from ship to ship* *They may walk on their hind legs*
Puli	*Group:* Herding *Purpose:* Herder Sheep Guard Dog	25-40 lbs. 15- 18 inch	++ ***	Elbow Dysplasia Hip Dysplasia Patella Luxation	Mesomorphic	**Agility** Guard Dog **Herding** Jog - Great **Obedience Training** Watch Dog	Loves to swim, reserved w/ strangers, energetic, very protective, brave, independent, willful, quick-tempered, dominant, obedient *Working Dog: Needs to have a job to do to keep mentally and physically stimulated* *Bred to herd and guard livestock during the day*

Medium Breed	Group / Purpose for breeding	Size Lb.. / Ht./ inch	Activity Level+ ---------- Exercise Needs*	Suggested Orthopedic OFA Tests	Body Type	Sport or Activity	More Information
Saluki	**Group:** Hound **Purpose:** Hunter Rabbit Gazelle Fox Sight - Hound	31-55 lbs. 23-28 inch	++ ****	Hip Dysplasia	Ectomorphic	Agility, Watch Dog, Tracking, Hunting, Racing, Lure Coursing, Jog - Good	*Do not trust w/ non-canine pets* Reserved w/ strangers, friendly, loves to run, fast, distractible, sensitive, skittish, submissive, graceful. *Can jump over fences as high as 7'.* *One of the oldest breed of domestic dog found mummified in Egyptian tombs as far back as 2100 BC*
Samoyed	**Group:** Working **Purpose:** Sled Dog Herder Reindeer	40-75 lbs. 19-23.5 inch	+++ ***	Hip Dysplasia	Mesomorphic	Canicross, Carting, Herding, Jog - Great, Skijoring, Sledding / Mushing, Watch Dog	*Can be Dog Aggressive, esp. same sex dogs. Do not trust w/ non-canine pets* Reserved with strangers, likes to roam, likes to chew, gentle, dignified, easy going, friendly, playful, willful. *Also bred to keep owner warm at night. May try to 'herd' kids and other pets*
Siberian Husky	**Group:** Working **Purpose:** Sled Dog	35-60 lbs. 20-23.5 inch	+++ ****	Elbow Dysplasia Hip Dysplasia	Mesomorphic	Agility, Bikejoring, Canicross, Carting, Jog - Great, Skijoring, Sledding / Mushing, Therapy Dog	Mischievous, willful, likes the cold, likes to roam, easily bored, sociable, easy going, patient. *Working Dog: Needs to have a job to do to keep mentally and physically stimulated. Howls*
Soft-Coated Wheaten Terrier	**Group:** Terrier **Purpose:** Hunter Ratter Herder Guard Dog	30-40 lbs. 17-19 inch	++ ***	Elbow Dysplasia Hip Dysplasia	Mesomorphic	Agility, Guard Dog, Herding, Jog - Great, Performing Tricks, Tracking, Watch Dog	Graceful, strong, playful, easy-going, self-confident, alert, well-coordinated, energetic. *Not as aggressive as some other terriers*

Medium Breed	Group / Purpose for breeding	Size Lb.. / Ht./ inch	Activity Level+ ---------- Exercise Needs*	Suggested Orthopedic OFA Tests	Body Type	Sport or Activity	More Information
Staffordshire Bull Terrier	*Group:* Terrier *Purpose:* Bull Baiting Hunter Ratter Badger	24-38 lbs. 14-16 inch	++ ***	Elbow Dysplasia Hip Dysplasia Patella Luxation	Endomorphic	Carting Hunting Jog - OK Obedience Training Performing Tricks Watch Dog Weight Pulling	*Can be Dog Aggressive, esp. same sex dogs. Do not trust w/ non-canine pets* Likes to dig and chew, high pain tolerance, courageous, willful, impulsive, devoted, strong prey drive, friendly w/ strangers, tends to be combative w/ unknown dogs. *Not a strong swimmer* *Great family dog if raised properly and purchased from a reputable breeder*
Standard Schnauzer	*Group:* Working *Purpose:* Hunter Ratter Guard Dog	28 lbs. 17.5-19.5 inch	+++ ***	Hip Dysplasia	Mesomorphic	Agility Canicross Disc Dog Flyball Guard Dog Herding Hunting Jog - Great Obedience Training Retrieving Tracking Watch Dog	*Can be Dog Aggressive Do not trust w/ non-canine pets* Reserved with strangers, no doggy odor, fearless, willful, spirited, demanding, energetic, protective, can be dominant, reliable, high endurance *Used to accompany coaches and as a messenger in WWI*
Sussex Spaniel	*Group:* Sporting *Purpose:* Hunter Bird Small Game	35-50 lbs. 13-15 inch	++ **	No Information Available	Micromelic Achondroplasia	Hunting Jog - OK Retrieving Tracking Watch Dog	*Can be Dog Aggressive* Steady, calm, gentle, devoted, willful, can be dominant *Bays and howls* *Used for hunting in the undergrowth*

Medium Breed	Group Purpose for breeding	Size Lbs. Ht./ inch	Activity Level+ ---------- Exercise Needs*	Suggested Orthopedic OFA Tests	Body Type	Sport or Activity	More Information
Vizsla	*Group:* Sporting *Purpose:* Hunter Bird Retriever Pointer	40-65 lbs. 21- 24 inch	++ ***	Elbow Dysplasia Hip Dysplasia Patellar Luxation	Mesomorphic Ectomorphic	Canicross Hunting Jog - Great Obedience Training Pointing Retrieving Tracking Watch Dog	Very loving, protective, gentle mannered , fearless, distractible, athletic, excellent swimmers, gets bored easily, high energy, likes to chew *Working Dog:* Needs to have a job to do to keep mentally and physically stimulated Wire hair recognized in Europe
Welsh Springer Spaniel	*Group:* Sporting *Purpose:* Hunter Bird Retriever	38- 48 lbs. 17-19 inch	++ ***	Elbow Dysplasia Hip Dysplasia	Mesomorphic	Canicross Hunting Jog - Great Retrieving Tracking Watch Dog	Reserved with strangers, fairly independent, great stamina, sensitive, active, loyal, can have 'selective hearing', easily bored *Working Dog:* Needs to have a job to do to keep mentally and physically stimulated

Large Breed	Group Purpose for breeding	Size Lbs. Ht./inch	Activity Level+ ---------- Exercise Needs*	Suggested Orthopedic OFA Tests	Body Types	Sport or Activity	More Information
 Afghan Hound	*Group:* Hound *Purpose:* Hunter Deer Goats Wolves Herder Sheep Watch Dog Sight- Hound	45-64 lbs. 24-28 inch	++ ****	Hip Dysplasia	Endomorphic	Agility Herding Hunting Jog - Great Lure Coursing Racing Tracking Watch Dog	*Can be Dog Aggressive* *Do not trust w/ non-canine pets* Reserved with strangers, dignified, noble, courageous, sensitive, loyal, aloof, clownish when playing, cat like tendencies, independent, may ignore commands
 Akita (American)	*Group:* Working *Purpose:* Hunter Deer Bear Sled Dog Guard Dog	75-100 lbs. 24-28 inch	++ ***	Elbow Dysplasia Hip Dysplasia Patella Luxation	Mesomorphic	Carting Guard Dog Hunting Jog - Good Sledding Tracking Watch Dog	*Can be Dog Aggressive* *Do not trust w/ non-canine pets* Reserved with strangers, docile, affectionate, fearless, courageous, extremely protective, can be food possessive , dominant *Can be aggressive with unknown dogs & children* *Working Dog: Needs to have a job to do to keep mentally and physically stimulated* *'Soft Mouthed'* *National Dog of Japan and National Monument (bronze statue)*
 Alaskan Malamute	*Group:* Working *Purpose:* Sled Dog Guard Dog	75-85 lbs. 23-25 inch	++ ***	Elbow Dysplasia Hip Dysplasia	Mesomorphic	Bikejoring Canicross Carting Guard Dog Jog - Great Search & Rescue Skijoring Sledding / Mushing Weight Pulling	*Can be Dog Aggressive, esp. same sex dogs* *Do not trust w/ non-canine pets* Prey driven, friendly, can be rambunctious, , loves the outdoors, great endurance *Howls* Needs to be part of a pack, whether other dogs or humans. If left outdoors year round, make sure they stay cool in the summer *Working Dog: Needs to have a job to do to keep mentally and physically stimulated*

Large Breed	Group Purpose for breeding	Size Lbs. ---------- Ht./ inch	Activity Level+ ---------- Exercise Needs*	Suggested Orthopedic OFA Tests	Body Types	Sport or Activity	More Information
American Foxhound	**Group:** Hound **Purpose:** Hunter Fox Scent-Hound	60-70 lbs. 21-25 inch	++ ***	No Information Available	Mesomorphic	**Agility** Hunting **Jog - Great** Tracking	*Do not trust w/ non-canine pets* Sweet, gentle, brave, good in the field, likes to roam, loyal, great stamina *The working breed & show/companion breeds have differences in their personalities. If you are looking for a companion, do not buy hounds that were bred as hunting dogs and vice versa* *Needs to be part of a pack, whether other dogs or humans* *Bays and howls* **Working Dog**: *Needs to have a job to do to keep mentally and physically stimulated*
Anatolian Shepherd Dog	**Group:** Working **Purpose:** Guard Dog Livestock	80-150 lbs. 27-30 inch	++ ***	Elbow Dysplasia Hip Dysplasia	Giant Mesomorphic	**Carting** Guard Dog **Jog - Good** Watch Dog	*Can be Dog Aggressive* Reserved with strangers, good w/kids and pets when raised together, dominant, protective, loyal, alert, steadfast, brave, very independent *Bred to think and act independently and to protect flock against predators* **Working Dog**: *Needs to have a job to do to keep mentally and physically stimulated*

Large Breed	Group / Purpose for breeding	Size Lbs. Ht./inch	Activity Level+ ---------- Exercise Needs*	Suggested Orthopedic OFA Tests	Body Types	Sport or Activity	More Information
Beauceron	**Group:** Herding **Purpose:** Herder Sheep	80-110 lbs. 24-27.5 inch	++ ****	Elbow Dysplasia Hip Dysplasia	Mesomorphic	Agility Bikejoring Canicross Guard Dog Herding Jog - Good Obedience Training Schutzhund / Ring Sports Tracking Watch Dog	*Can be Dog Aggressive* Wary of strangers, highly protective, very calm. brave, faithful, vigilant, fearless, patient, obedient, eager to please, good w/ kids if raised together *In both World Wars they were used as messengers, supply transport, to detect land mines and to rescue the wounded* *Working Dog: Needs to have a job to do to keep mentally and physically stimulated*
Belgian Groenendael **(Sheepdog)**	**Group:** Herding **Purpose:** Herder Sheep	45-65 lbs. 22-26 inch	++ ****	Elbow Dysplasia Hip Dysplasia	Mesomorphic	Agility Bikejoring Bomb Detection Canicross Flyball Guard Dog Herding Jog - Great Narcotic Detection Obedience Training Performing Tricks Schutzhund / Ring Sports Search & Rescue Skijoring Sledding / Mushing Tracking Watch Dog	*Can be Dog Aggressive* Obedient, serious, watchful, protective, territorial, active, loyal, obedient, proud, athletic, strong, imposing, dominant *'Belgian Shepherd'* *Needs to be part of the family, although will not be happy as a 'house dog'. Has separation anxiety if left alone for long periods of time* *May try to 'herd' kids and other pets* *Working Dog: Needs to have a job to do to keep mentally and physically stimulated*

Large Breed	Group Purpose for breeding	Size Lbs. Ht./ inch	Activity Level+ ---------- Exercise Needs*	Suggested Orthopedic OFA Tests	Body Types	Sport or Activity	More Information
Belgian Malinois	*Group:* Herding *Purpose:* Herding Sheep	40-75 lbs. 22-26 inch	++ ****	Elbow Dysplasia Hip Dysplasia	Mesomorphic	See Belgian Groenendael Above	*Can be Dog Aggressive* Responsive, confident, proud, very obedient, alert, devoted *'Belgian Shepherd'* *Needs to be part of the family, although will not be happy as a 'house dog'. Has separation anxiety if left alone for long periods of time* *May try to 'herd' kids and other pets* *Working Dog: Needs to have a job to do to keep mentally and physically stimulated*
Belgian Tervuren	*Group:* Herding *Purpose:* Herder Sheep	40-75 lbs. 22-26 inch	++ ****	Elbow Dysplasia Hip Dysplasia	Mesomorphic	Agility, Bikejoring, Bomb Detection, Canicross, Flyball, Guard Dog, Herding, Jog - Great, Narcotic Detection, Obedience Training, Performing Tricks, Schutzhund / Ring Sports, Search & Rescue, Skijoring, Sledding / Mushing, Tracking, Watch Dog	*Can be Dog Aggressive* Obedient, serious, watchful, protective, territorial, active, loyal, responsive, obedient *'Belgian Shepherd'* *Needs to be part of the family, although will not be happy as a 'house dog'. Has separation anxiety if left alone for long periods of time* *May try to 'herd' kids and other pets* *Working Dog: Needs to have a job to do to keep mentally and physically stimulated*

Large Breed	Group / Purpose for breeding	Size Lbs. / Ht./inch	Activity Level+ ---------- Exercise Needs*	Suggested Orthopedic OFA Tests	Body Types	Sport or Activity	More Information
Bernese Mountain Dog	*Group:* Working *Purpose:* Guard Dog	80-120 lbs. 23-27.5 inch	++ ****	Elbow Dysplasia Hip Dysplasia	Mesomorphic/ Endomorphic	Carting 'Drafting Trials' Guard Dog Herding Jog - Good Obedience Training Search & Rescue Tracking Watch Dog	Quiet, devoted, loyal, affectionate, gentle, alert, good-natured, self-confident; self-assured, active, does not have a great deal of endurance, faithful, stable, docile *Bred as draft dogs, pulling carts, driving cattle and to guard livestock* *Working Dog: Needs to have a job to do to keep mentally and physically stimulated*
Black and Tan Coonhound	*Group:* Hound *Purpose:* Hunter Raccoon Bear Deer Lg. Cats Scent-Hound	65-90 lbs. 23-27 inch	++ ****	Elbow Dysplasia Hip Dysplasia	Mesomorphic	Hunting Jog - Great Tracking Watch Dog	*Can be Dog Aggressive, esp. same sex dogs. Do not trust w/ non-canine pets* Likes to roam, reserved with strangers, dedicated worker, alert, eager, willful, gentle *Distracted by scents. Will howl if left alone for long periods* *Working Dog: Needs to have a job to do to keep mentally and physically stimulated*
Black Russian Terrier	*Group:* Working *Purpose:* Guard Dog Military Dog	75-130 lbs. 26-30 inch	++ ***	Elbow Dysplasia Hip Dysplasia	Mesomorphic	Agility Carting Guard Dog Jog - Great Obedience Training Performing Tricks Retrieving Schutzhund / Ring Sports Search & Rescue Sledding / Mushing Tracking Watch Dog	*Can be Dog Aggressive* Loyal, brave, calm, self-confident, protective, can be stubborn, highly intelligent, needs to be w/ people *May try to 'herd' kids and other pets* *Working Dog: Needs to have a job to do to keep mentally and physically stimulated*

Large Breed	Group Purpose for breeding	Size Lbs. Ht./ inch	Activity Level+ ----------- Exercise Needs*	Suggested Orthopedic OFA Tests	Body Types	Sport or Activity	More Information
Bloodhound	**Group:** Hound **Purpose:** Hunter Scent - Hound	80-110 lbs. 23-27 inch	**++** *******	Elbow Dysplasia Hip Dysplasia Patella Luxation	Mesomorphic	Hunting Jog - Great Narcotic Detection Search & Rescue Tracking Watch Dog	*Can be Dog Aggressive, esp. same sex dogs. Do not trust w/ non-canine pets* Noble, kind, patient, friendly, good natured, docile, energetic, stubborn, has good endurance, easily distracted by scents *Drools & Bays Strong 'doggy odor'* **Working Dog**: *Needs to have a job to do to keep mentally and physically stimulated*
Boerboel **AKA South African Mastiff**	**Group:** Working **Purpose:** Guard Dog	150-200 lbs. 23-28 inch	**++** *******	Elbow Dysplasia Hip Dysplasia	Endomorphic	Carting Guard Dog Jog - OK/Good Watch Dog Weight Pulling	The Boerboel is a dominant and intelligent dog with strong protective instincts and a willingness to please. When approached is calm, stable and confident, at times displaying a self-assured aloofness. He should recognize a threat or lack thereof. He is loving with children and family.
Borzoi	**Group:** Hound **Purpose:** Hunter Wolves Sight - Hound	60-105 lbs. 26-28 inch	**++** ********	Elbow Dysplasia Hip Dysplasia	Ectomorphic	Agility Hunting Jog - Great Lure Coursing Obedience Training Racing	*"Russian Wolfhound" Can be Dog Aggressive Do not trust w/ non-canine pets* Very fast, sweet, not demanding, noble, cat-like, silent, docile, can be snappish, couch potato, gentle, slow to learn new commands, high prey drive, no traffic/safety awareness *Due to their breeding, they may chase after any animal and seize it at the neck to immobilize* *Should eat small meals*

Large Breed	Group Purpose for breeding	Size Lbs. Ht./ inch	Activity Level+ ---------- Exercise Needs*	Suggested Orthopedic OFA Tests	Body Types	Sport or Activity	More Information
Bouvier des Flandres	*Group:* Herding *Purpose:* Herder Sheep Cattle Guard Dog	75-110 lbs. 23-27.5 inch	++ ****	Elbow Dysplasia Hip Dysplasia	Mesomorphic/ Endomorphic	**Agility** Carting **Guard Dog** Guide Dog - Blind **Herding** Jog - Great **Obedience Training** Schutzhund / Ring Sports **Search & Rescue** Tracking **Watch Dog** Weight Pulling	*Can be Dog Aggressive* Reserved with strangers, brave, pleasant nature, calm, gentle, loyal, responsible, rational, protective, has complex self-control *Used as a message carrier and rescue dog during WWI* *May try to 'herd' kids and other pets* *Working Dog: Needs to have a job to do to keep mentally and physically stimulated*
Boxer	*Group:* Working *Purpose:* Guard Dog Bull Baiting	60-70 lbs. 21-25 inch	++ ***	Hip Dysplasia	Mesomorphic	**Agility** Bikejoring **Canicross** Carting **Guard Dog** Jog - Great **Obedience Training** Performing Tricks **Schutzhund / Ring Sports** Search & Rescue **Therapy Dog** Watch Dog	*Can be Dog Aggressive* Very clean, playful, energetic, devoted, alert, protective, obedient, can be headstrong, suspicious of strangers *Drools and snores* *The breed gets its name by his tendency to play by standing on its hind legs and boxing with its front paws* *Used as messenger dog, pack-carrier, attack dog and guard dog during WWI* *Working Dog: Needs to have a job to do to keep mentally and physically stimulated*

Large Breed	Group Purpose for breeding	Size Lbs. Ht./ inch	Activity Level+ ---------- Exercise Needs*	Suggested Orthopedic OFA Tests	Body Types	Sport or Activity	More Information
Briard	**Group:** Herding **Purpose:** Herder Sheep Guard Dog	60-90 lbs. 22-27 inch	++ ****	Elbow Dysplasia Hip Dysplasia	*Mesomorphic*	Agility Bikejoring Canicross Guard Dog Herding Jog - Great Search & Rescue Watch Dog	*Can be Dog Aggressive* Reserved with strangers, brave, loyal, fearless, sweet, headstrong, excellent hearing, willful, good w/kids when raised together, good memory, protective, willful *"This breed was used by the French Army as a sentry, messenger, and to search for wounded soldiers because of its fine sense of hearing." (Wikipedia)* *May try to 'herd' kids and other pets* *Working Dog: Needs to have a job to do to keep mentally and physically stimulated*
Bullmastiff	**Group:** Working **Purpose:** Guard Dog	100-130 lbs. 24-27 inch	++ **	Elbow Dysplasia Hip Dysplasia	Endomorphic	Guard Dog Jog - OK/Good Tracking Watch Dog Weight Pulling	*Can be Dog Aggressive, esp. same sex dogs. Do not trust w/ non-canine pets* Reserved with strangers, good with kids/pets when raised together, good natured, willful, fearless, protective, docile, very powerful, loyal, muscular, fast, agile *Drools and snores* *Bred to help English wardens or gamekeepers guard estates and to track, tackle & hold down poachers* *More aggressive than the Mastiff*
Cane Corso **AKA Italian Mastiff**	**Group:** Working **Purpose:** Guard Dog	90-120 lbs. 23 -27 inch	++ ***	Elbow Dysplasia Hip Dysplasia Patella Luxation	Mesomorphic/ Endomorphic	Agility Guard Dog Jog - Good Tracking Watch Dog Weight Pulling	The Cane Corso as a protector of his property and owners is unequaled. Intelligent, he is easily trained. Noble, majestic and powerful his, presence is impressive. He is docile and affectionate to his owner, loving with children and family.

Large Breed	Group Purpose for breeding	Size Lbs. Ht./ inch	Activity Level+ ---------- Exercise Needs*	Suggested Orthopedic OFA Tests	Body Types	Sport or Activity	More Information
Chesapeake Bay Retriever	**Group:** Sporting **Purpose:** Hunter Bird Retriever	55-80 lbs. 21-26 inch	++ ****	Elbow Dysplasia Hip Dysplasia	Mesomorphic	Agility Bikejoring Canicross Dock Diving Guard Dog Hunting Jog - Great Obedience Training Retrieving Tracking Watch Dog	*Can be Dog Aggressive* Reserved with strangers, willful, loves to swim and be outdoors, courageous, protective, happy nature, territorial *Can be more aggressive than other retrievers* *Temperament is inherited, so choose carefully when picking a pup* *Some have a 'smile' bearing front teeth that is not aggressive*
Rough **Smooth** **Collie** (Rough and Smooth Coat)	**Group:** Herding **Purpose:** Herder Sheep Cattle Guard Dog	50-75 lbs. 22-26 inch	++ ***	N/A	Mesomorphic	Agility Bikejoring Canicross Disc Dog Flyball Guard Dog Guide Dog - Blind Herding Jog - Great Obedience Training Search & Rescue Therapy Dog Tracking Watch Dog	Noble, sensitive, sweet, kind, devoted, loyal, protective, easily housebroken, can be willful, energetic, great stamina *The herding breed & show/companion breeds have differences in their personalities. If you are looking for a companion, do not buy collies that were bred for herding and vice versa* *May try to 'herd' kids and other pets* *Nose can get easily sunburned*

Large Breed	Group Purpose for breeding	Size Lbs. Ht./ inch	Activity Level+ ---------- Exercise Needs*	Suggested Orthopedic OFA Tests	Body Types	Sport or Activity	More Information
Curly Coated Retriever	*Group:* Sporting *Purpose:* Hunter Bird Retriever	50-90 lbs. 23-27 inch	++ ****	Elbow Dysplasia Hip Dysplasia	Mesomorphic	Agility Dock Diving Flyball Guard Dog Hunting Jog - Great Obedience Training Retrieving Therapy Dog Tracking Watch Dog	Loves to swim, loyal, eager to please, confident, clever, mischievous, reserved with strangers, easily bored, active, calm in the household, agile, good endurance *'Soft mouthed'* *Working Dog: Needs to have a job to do to keep mentally and physically stimulated*
Doberman Pinscher	*Group:* Working *Purpose:* Guard Dog	60-75 lbs. 24-28 inch	+++ ****	Elbow Dysplasia Hip Dysplasia	Mesomorphic	Agility Guard Dog Jog - Great Obedience Training Schutzhund / Ring Sports Search & Rescue Watch Dog	*Dog Aggressive* Good when raised with kids, energetic, strong, fearless, assertive, determined, loyal, watchful, protective, can be dominant *Temperament is inherited, so choose carefully when picking a pup* *Working Dog: Needs to have a job to do to keep mentally and physically stimulated* *North American breeds tend to be calmer than European breeds*
Dogo Argentino	*Group:* Working *Purpose:* Hunt Large Game Boar	90-100 lbs. 24 -26 inch	++ ****	Elbow Dysplasia Hip Dysplasia	Mesomorphic	Agility Guard Dog Jog – Good Hunting Tracking Watch Dog	*The Dogo is a strong, tenacious and rustic dog that was created to protect family and property, as well as to hunt large game and destructive predators. He is a faithful companion at home and in the field. Of all of the Dogo's attributes, he is above all else, courageous.*

Large Breed	Group **Purpose for breeding**	Size Lbs. Ht./ inch	Activity Level+ ---------- Exercise Needs*	*Suggested Orthopedic OFA Tests*	**Body Types**	*Sport or Activity*	*More Information*
Dogue de Bordeaux AKA French Mastiff	*Group:* Working *Purpose:* Guard Dog Bull Baiting Herder Cattle	100-120 lbs. 23-27 inch	++ ***	Elbow Dysplasia Hip Dysplasia Patella Luxation	Endomorphic	Carting Guard Dog Jog - OK Watch Dog Weight Pulling	'French Mastiff' *Dog Aggressive* Good when raised with kid & pets, loyal, patient, devoted, stubborn *Drools and snores* *Needs a dominant owner* *Dams usually need a cesarean section for birthing*
English Foxhound	*Group:* Hound *Purpose:* Hunter Fox Scent - Hound	70-75 lbs. 23-24 inch	+++ ****	No Information Available	Mesomorphic	Agility Hunting Jog - Great Tracking Watch Dog	*Do not trust w/ non-canine pets* Active, bold, gentle, passionate, good in the field, likes to roam, social *The hunting breed & show/companion breeds have differences in their personalities. If you are looking for a companion, do not buy hounds that were bred for hunting and vice versa* *Does best with a 'pack' of other dogs* *Tends to bay* *Stockier and slower than the American Foxhound*
English Setter	Group: Sporting Purpose: Hunter Bird	50-70 lbs. 24-25 inch	++ ****	Elbow Dysplasia Hip Dysplasia	Mesomorphic	Agility Bikejoring Canicross Hunting Jog - Great Obedience Training Pointing Retrieving Tracking Watch Dog	Gentle, placid, friendly, likes to roam, can be hard to housebreak, digger, likes to jump, mild mannered, sensitive, enjoys playing with other dogs, energetic *Inside they are a lap dog and love to cuddle* *Working Dog: Needs to have a job to do to keep mentally and physically stimulated*

Large Breed	Group Purpose for breeding	Size Lbs. Ht./ inch	Activity Level+ ---------- Exercise Needs*	Suggested Orthopedic OFA Tests	Body Types	Sport or Activity	More Information
Flat-Coated Retriever	*Group:* Sporting *Purpose:* Hunter Bird	60-70 lbs. 22-24.5 inch	++ ****	Hip Dysplasia Patella Luxation	Mesomorphic	Agility Bikejoring Canicross Dock Diving Hunting Jog - Great Obedience Training Retrieving Skijoring Therapy Dog Tracking	Very friendly, loves to swim and roam, stable, smart, active, easily bored, outgoing, eager to please, very playful, enthusiastic *Although good w/ small children, may be very enthusiastic around them trying to play and may knock them down 'Flat-coated kiss' – where they tend to lick each other's mouth as a form of greeting* 'Soft mouthed'
German Shepherd	*Group:* Herding *Purpose:* Herder Sheep	55-90 lbs. 22-26 inch	++ ****	Elbow Dysplasia Hip Dysplasia	Mesomorphic	Agility Bomb / Accelerant Detection Disc Dog Flyball Guard Dog Guide Dog - Blind Herding Jog - Great Narcotic Detection Obedience Training Performing Tricks Schutzhund / Ring Sports Search & Rescue Sledding/ Mushing Therapy Dog Tracking Watch Dog	*May try to bite smaller dogs* Reserved with strangers, fearless, eager, alert, bold, cheerful, obedient, loyal, calm, confident, highly intelligent, can be overprotective of their family *Different lines vary in temperament and look, for example East German, West German, American* *Working Dog:* *Needs to have a job to do to keep mentally and physically stimulated*

Large Breed	Group **Purpose for breeding**	Size Lbs. Ht./inch	Activity Level+ ---------- Exercise Needs*	Suggested Orthopedic OFA Tests	Body Types	Sport or Activity	More Information
German Shorthaired Pointer	**Group:** Sporting **Purpose:** Hunter 　See Info. Retriever Pointer	45-70 lbs. 21-25 inch	+++ ****	Elbow Dysplasia Hip Dysplasia	Mesomorphic	Agility Bikejoring Canicross Dock Diving Hunting Jog - Great Obedience Training Pointing Retrieving Skijoring Tracking	*Can be Dog Aggressive* Reserved with strangers, gets bored easily, best with athletic family, very energetic, eager to please, friendly, loyal, protective, good with kids/pets if raised together, fun, likes to swim and roam, can jump fences from 4-6 feet high *Can hunt on both land and water for most any game on any terrain* *Working Dog: Needs to have a job to do to keep mentally and physically stimulated*
German Wirehaired Pointer	**Group:** Sporting **Purpose:** Hunter 　See Info. Retriever Pointer	50-75 lbs. 22-26 inch	+++ ****	Elbow Dysplasia Hip Dysplasia	Mesomorphic	Agility Bikejoring Canicross Hunting Jog - Great Pointing Retrieving Skijoring Tracking Watch Dog	*Can be Dog Aggressive* Reserved with strangers, can be jealous, vigorous, thoughtful, serious, can be high strung, willful, affectionate, eager to learn, likes to roam, very active *Can hunt on both land and water for most any game on any terrain* *Working Dog: Needs to have a job to do to keep mentally and physically stimulated*
Giant Schnauzer	**Group:** Working **Purpose:** Herder Cattle Military	50-75 lbs. 23.5-27.5 inch	++ ****	Elbow Dysplasia Hip Dysplasia	Mesomorphic	Agility Carting Guard Dog Jog - Great Obedience Training Schutzhund / Ring Sports Tracking Watch Dog Weight Pulling	*Dog Aggressive* Reserved w/ strangers, good with kids when raised together, protective, bold, spirited, loyal, responsible, dominant, powerful *Working Dog: Needs to have a job to do to keep mentally and physically stimulated*

Large Breed	Group Purpose for breeding	Size Lbs. Ht./ inch	Activity Level+ ---------- Exercise Needs*	Suggested Orthopedic OFA Tests	Body Types	Sport or Activity	More Information
Golden Retriever	*Group:* Sporting *Purpose:* Hunter Bird Retriever	60-75 lbs. 21.5-24 inch	++ ***	Elbow Dysplasia Hip Dysplasia	Mesomorphic	**Agility** Bikejoring **Canicross** Dock Diving **Guide Dog - Blind** Hunting **Jog - Great** Narcotic Detection **Obedience Training** Retrieving **Search & Rescue** Therapy Dog **Tracking** Watch Dog	Very friendly, stable, loyal, confident, easily bored, outgoing, eager to please, patient, can be distractible, kind, love the water *Great hunting dog both on land and water* *'Soft mouthed'*
Gordon Setter	*Group:* Sporting *Purpose:* Hunter Bird Retriever Pointer	45-80 lbs. 24-26 inch	+++ ****	Elbow Dysplasia Hip Dysplasia	Mesomorphic	**Agility** Bikejoring **Canicross** Guard Dog **Hunting** Jog - Great **Pointing** Retrieving **Tracking** Watch Dog	*Can be Dog Aggressive* Reserved w/ strangers, devoted, polite, gentle, courageous, willful, likes to roam, alert, interested, eager to learn, loyal, thrive attention *Slow to mature – do not over exercise or start agility training until at least 18 months old* *Can be distracted by scents, so do not allow to roam free*

Large Breed	Group Purpose for breeding	Size Lbs. Ht./ inch	Activity Level+ ---------- Exercise Needs*	Suggested Orthopedic OFA Tests	Body Types	Sport or Activity	More Information
Great Dane	*Group:* Working *Purpose:* Guard Dog Hunter Boar	120-150 lbs. 28-30 inch	++ ****	Hip Dysplasia	Giant Mesomorphic/ Endomorphic	**Carting** **Guard Dog** **Hunting** **Jog - Good** **Tracking** **Watch Dog**	*Can be Dog Aggressive* 'Gentle Giant', Kind, dignified, sweet, brave, loyal, friendly nature *Because of size, early training is very important* *Slow to mature; Do not jog or do vigorous exercise until at least 12-18 months old*
Great Pyrenees	*Group:* Working *Purpose:* Guard Dog Livestock	85-130 lbs. 25-32 inch	++ ***	Elbow Dysplasia Hip Dysplasia Patella Luxation	Giant Mesomorphic/ Endomorphic	**Carting** **Guard Dog** **Jog - OK** **Sledding/ Mushing** **Therapy Dog** **Watch Dog** **Weight Pulling**	*Can be Dog Aggressive* Good when raised w/ pets, courageous, calm, protective, territorial, serious, powerful, independent *Working Dog: Needs to have a job to do to keep mentally and physically stimulated*
Greater Swiss Mountain Dog	*Group:* Working *Purpose:* Guard Dog	85-145 lbs. 23.5-27 inch	++ ***	Elbow Dysplasia Hip Dysplasia Patella Luxation	Mesomorphic	**Carting** **Guard Dog** **Herding** **Jog - OK/Good** **Obedience Training** **Search & Rescue** **Tracking** **Watch Dog** **Weight Pulling**	May chase other pets, watchful, protective, eager to please, adoring, loyal, even tempered *Bred as a 'butcher's dog and to pull carts and later to drive cattle* *Working Dog: Needs to have a job to do to keep mentally and physically stimulated*
Greyhound	*Group:* Hound *Purpose:* Hunter Racing Sight -Hound	60-70 lbs. 26-30 inch	+/++ ***	N/A	Ectomorphic	**Agility** **Watch Dog** **Obedience Training** **Hunting** **Therapy Dog** **Racing** **Lure Coursing** **Jog – Good**	*Do not trust w/ non-canine pets* Sweet, high prey drive, sensitive, elegant, loyal, willful, likes to be w/ the 'pack', 'couch potato' *Do not use flea collars* *Fastest dog w/ speeds up to 43 MPH* *One of the oldest breeds of dog*

Large Breed	Group / Purpose for breeding	Size Lbs. Ht./ inch	Activity Level+ ---------- Exercise Needs*	Suggested Orthopedic OFA Tests	Body Types	Sport or Activity	More Information
Irish Setter	**Group:** Sporting **Purpose:** Hunter Bird Retriever Pointer	60-70 lbs. 24-28 inch	++ ****	Hip Dysplasia	Mesomorphic	Agility Bikejoring Canicross Hunting Jog - Great Pointing Retrieving Tracking Watch Dog	Giddy, lovable, impulsive, outgoing, thrives on activity, fast, good endurance, energetic, happy, tendency to 'play deaf' *Working Dog: Needs to have a job to do to keep mentally and physically stimulated* Needs people; not a good dog for someone who plans to be away or keep them in a kennel or yard.
Irish Wolfhound	**Group:** Hound **Purpose:** Hunter Wolves Sight -Hound	105-130 lbs. 30-36 inch	++ ****	Elbow Dysplasia Hip Dysplasia	Giant Ectomorphic	Agility Guard Dog Hunting Jog - Good Lure Coursing Racing Tracking	Fast and likes to chase, gentle, patient, sweet, loyal, may 'course' kids/pets, clumsy, reliable, generous, thoughtful *Tallest breed of dog* Guard dog because of size, not demeanor Slow to mature: Do not over exercise, run or lure coursing until 18 months.
Komondor	**Group:** Working **Purpose:** Guard Dog Livestock	80 -100 lbs. 27-30 inch	++ ***	Hip Dysplasia	Mesomorphic	Guard Dog Jog - Good Watch Dog	*Can be Dog Aggressive* Wary of strangers, very protective, can be aggressive, very territorial, willful, easily bored, not a great family dog, respectful of master, responsible *Thinks and acts independently* *The dog will knock down the intruder until the owner returns. Will usually sleep during the day and patrol at night* *Working Dog: Needs to have a job to do to keep mentally and physically stimulated*

Large Breed	Group Purpose for breeding	Size Lbs. Ht./ inch	Activity Level+ ---------- Exercise Needs*	Suggested Orthopedic OFA Tests	Body Types	Sport or Activity	More Information
Kuvasz	**Group:** Working **Purpose:** Guard Dog Hunter Bear Wild Boar	70-115 lbs. 26-30 inch	++ ****	Elbow Dysplasia Hip Dysplasia Patella Luxation	Mesomorphic	Carting Guard Dog Hunter Jog - Great Watch Dog	*Can be Dog Aggressive* Wary of strangers, curious, bold, determined, brave, very protective, can be aggressive, will defend his territory fiercely *Bred to think independently* *Do not leave unsupervised with unfamiliar animals/kids*
Labrador Retriever	**Group:** Sporting **Purpose:** Hunter Bird Retriever	65-80 lbs. 21-24 inch	++ ***	Elbow Dysplasia Hip Dysplasia	Mesomorphic	Agility Bikejoring Canicross Carting Dock Diving Guide Dog - Blind Hunting Jog - Great Narcotic Detection Obedience Training Retrieving Search & Rescue Service Dog Sledding / Mushing Therapy Dog Tracking Watch Dog	Loves to swim, friendly, stable, loyal, confident, high spirited, eager to please, patient, strong necks that may pull on lead *Do not overfeed* *Bred to jump overboard into the water and haul fishing nets*

Large Breed	Group Purpose for breeding	Size Lbs. Ht./ inch	Activity Level+ ---------- Exercise Needs*	Suggested Orthopedic OFA Tests	Body Types	Sport or Activity	More Information
Mastiff (English) AKA Old English Mastiff	*Group:* Working *Purpose:* Guard Dog Bull Baiting	150-200 lbs. 27.5-30 inch	++ ***	Elbow Dysplasia Hip Dysplasia Patella Luxation	Giant Endomorphic	**Carting** Guard Dog **Jog - Good** Watch Dog **Weight Pulling**	Good with pets when raised together, good natured, calm, steady, docile, brave loyal, protective *Drools, wheezes and snores* *Working Dog: Needs to have a job to do to keep mentally and physically stimulated*
Neapolitan Mastiff	*Group:* Working *Purpose:* Guard Dog	110-200 lbs. 24-31 inch	+ ***	Elbow Dysplasia Hip Dysplasia	Giant Endomorphic	**Carting** Guard Dog **Jog - No/OK** Watch Dog **Weight Pulling**	*Can be Dog Aggressive* Good with kids/pets when raised together, wary of strangers, extremely protective, fearless, peaceful, steady *Bred to fight alongside Roman Legions* *Working Dog: Needs to have a job to do to keep mentally and physically stimulated*
Newfoundland	*Group:* Working *Purpose:* Retriever Rescue Water	100-150 lbs. 26-28 inch	++ ***	Elbow Dysplasia Hip Dysplasia	Giant Endomorphic	**Carting** Guard Dog **Jog - Great** Obedience Training **Retrieving** Search & Rescue **Watch Dog** Water Rescue **Weight Pulling**	Loves to swim, noble, calm, gentle, very devoted, peaceable, sociable, protective, loyal, courageous *Possibly the strongest yet gentlest breeds* *Bred to haul in nets, retriever articles that fell overboard and for water rescue* *Partly webbed feet and water-resistant coat*

Large Breed	Group Purpose for breeding	Size Lbs. Ht./ inch	Activity Level+ ---------- Exercise Needs*	Suggested Orthopedic OFA Tests	Body Types	Sport or Activity	More Information
Old English Sheepdog	*Group:* Herding *Purpose:* Herder Sheep	60-100 lbs. 21-22 inch	++ ***	Hip Dysplasia	Mesomorphic	Carting Herding Jog - Great Obedience Training Retrieving Watch Dog	Even tempered, adaptable, gentle, friendly, faithful, 'couch potato, can be strong willed, bubbly *May try to 'herd' kids and other pets by bumping into them* *Working Dog: Needs to have a job to do to keep mentally and physically stimulated* *Farmers sheered the dog when sheering their sheep to make blankets, etc.*
Otterhound	*Group:* Hound *Purpose:* Hunter Otter Mink Raccoon	100-115 lbs. 24-27 inch	++ ***	Elbow Dysplasia Hip Dysplasia	Mesomorphic	Hunting Jog - Great 'Swimming' Tracking Watch Dog	*Do not trust with non-canine pets,* Great swimmer, likes to roam, bold, boisterous, devoted, willful, loving *Likes to bay and snores* *Able to swim for hours without stopping*
Pointer	*Group:* Sporting *Purpose:* Hunter Bird Hare Pointer	45-75 lbs. 23-28 inch	++ ****	Elbow Dysplasia Hip Dysplasia	Mesomorphic	Bikejoring Canicross Hunting Jog - Great Obedience Training Pointing Tracking	Reserved with strangers, energetic, high endurance, enthusiastic hunter, calm, distractible, good w/ kids when raised together *Not a great swimmer* *Can be a couch potato, although does require regular exercise, preferably a jog twice a day and a fenced backyard*

Large | Dog Breed Chart

Large Breed	Group / Purpose for breeding	Size Lbs. / Ht./inch	Activity Level+ ---------- Exercise Needs*	Suggested Orthopedic OFA Tests	Body Types	Sport or Activity	More Information
Poodle (Standard)	*Group:* Non-Sporting *Purpose:* Hunter Bird Retriever	45-65 lbs. 22-26 inch	++ ****	Hip Dysplasia	Mesomorphic	Agility Canicross Dock Diving Guard Dog Hunting Jog - Great Obedience Training Performing Tricks Pointing Retrieving 'Swimming' Tracking Watch Dog	Extremely intelligent, dignified, good natured, proud, pleasant, sensitive, likes to swim, mischievous, easily bored, loves people Bred as a water dog – good at many water sports One of the most intelligent and trainable breeds Although some state that the show clip is actually a working clip where the joints are covered to protect from the cold water, some skeptics asked why other breeds do not need this same clip. The clip may have possibly come from their days as circus performers
Presa Canario AKA Canarian Dog	*Group:* Foundation *Purpose:* Guard Dog *Home*	70-120 lbs. 22 -26 inch	++ ***	Hip Dysplasia	Mesomorphic/ Endomorphic	Agility Guard Dog Jog - Good Tracking Watch Dog Weight Pulling	The standard of the breed states: "their aspect denotes power. Severe gaze. Especially gifted for the function of guard and defense and traditionally for the conduction of cattle. Impetuous temperament, skilled fighter, low and deep bark. He is gentle and noble in family and distrustful with the strangers.
Rhodesian Ridgeback	*Group:* Hound *Purpose:* Hunter Lions Guard Dog Retriever	65-75 lbs. 24-27 inch	++ ***	Elbow Dysplasia Hip Dysplasia	Mesomorphic	Agility Bikejoring Canicross Hunting Jog - Great Tracking Watch Dog	'African Lion Hound' *Can be Dog Aggressive, esp. same sex dogs. Do not trust w/ non-canine pets* Good hunter, calm, good natured, can be dominant, aloof w/ strangers, fast Used in packs to distract lions while waiting for their master to make the kill. Can withstand high temperatures and go without food and water for over 24 hours (although not recommended) Tick resistant coat. *Working Dog:* Needs to have a job to do to keep mentally and physically stimulated

Large Breed	Group / Purpose for breeding	Size Lbs. / Ht./ inch	Activity Level+ ---------- Exercise Needs*	Suggested Orthopedic OFA Tests	Body Types	Sport or Activity	More Information
Rottweiler	**Group:** Working **Purpose:** Guard Dog Herder Cattle	100-115 lbs. 22-27 inch	++ ***	Elbow Dysplasia Hip Dysplasia	Mesomorphic/ Endomorphic	Carting Guard Dog Guide Dog - Blind Herding Jog - Great Obedience Training Schutzhund / Ring Sports Search & Rescue Service Dog Tracking Watch Dog Weight Pulling	*Can be Dog Aggressive, esp. same sex dogs.* Reserved with strangers, good w/ kids & pets when raised together, dominant, devoted, courageous, protective, powerful, obedient, eager to work *Needs a dominant owner* ***Working Dog:*** *Needs to have a job to do to keep mentally and physically stimulated*
Scottish Deerhound	**Group:** Hound **Purpose:** Hunter Deer Sight - Hound	75-110 lbs. 28-30 inch	++ ****	Hip Dysplasia	Ectomorphic	Agility Hunting Jog - Good Lure Coursing Racing	***Do not trust w/ non-canine pets*** Fast and likes to chase, gentle, quiet, peaceable, willful, well behaved, can be slow to obey commands, extremely friendly *Needs a large safe area to run*
Spinone Italiano	**Group:** Sporting **Purpose:** Hunter Pointer Retriever	62-86 lbs. 22-25 inch	++ ***	Elbow Dysplasia Hip Dysplasia	Mesomorphic	Agility Hunting Jog - Good Obedience Training Performing Tricks Pointing Retrieving Tracking Watch Dog	Reserved with strangers, easy going, docile, likes to swim, reserved, stubborn, calm, 'slobbers', gentle natured, trots at a slow pace' loves people and other dogs *Versatile hunter*

Large Breed	Group Purpose for breeding	Size Lbs. Ht./ inch	Activity Level+ ----------- Exercise Needs*	Suggested Orthopedic OFA Tests	Body Types	Sport or Activity	More Information
  St. Bernard	*Group:* Working *Purpose:* Rescue	130-200 lbs. 25.5-27.5 inch	+ ****	Elbow Dysplasia Hip Dysplasia	Giant Endomorphic	Carting Jog - Good Search & Rescue Watch Dog Weight Pulling	Good with kids/pets when raised together, calm, dignified, obedient, steady, kind, patient *Be careful with small children because of size* *Short hair breed is used for cold temperatures, as the long hair tend to get icicles* *Drools, wheezes and snores*
  Tibetan Mastiff	*Group:* Working *Purpose:* Guard Dog Livestock	130-200 lbs. 24-26 inch	+ ****	Elbow Dysplasia Hip Dysplasia	Giant Endomorphic	Guard Dog Jog - OK Watch Dog	*Can be Dog Aggressive* Good with kids/pets when raised together, reserved w/ strangers, highly protective, *jogging may be hard on their joints,* territorial, brave, noble, fearless, stubborn *Guards at night and sleeps during the day* *Asian breeds are more protective and aggressive than Western breeds*
  Weimaraner	*Group:* Sporting *Purpose:* Hunter Boar Bear Fox Rabbits Fowl Pointer Tracker	55-85 lbs. 23-27 inch	++ ***	Elbow Dysplasia Hip Dysplasia	Mesomorphic	Agility Bikejoring Canicross Flyball Guard Dog Hunting Jog - Great Pointing Retrieving Search & Rescue Service Dog Tracking Watch Dog	*Can be Dog Aggressive, esp. same sex dogs. Do not trust w/ non-canine pets* Reserved with strangers, happy, rambunctious, willful, quick learner, high prey drive, fast, territorial, powerful *All purpose gun dog* *Best with an athletic family able to keep up w/ their active lifestyle* *Known to have separation anxiety* *Working Dog: Needs to have a job to do to keep mentally and physically stimulated*

Large Breed	Group Purpose for breeding	Size Lbs. Ht./ inch	Activity Level+ ---------- Exercise Needs*	Suggested Orthopedic OFA Tests	Body Types	Sport or Activity	More Information
Wirehaired Pointing Griffon	*Group:* Sporting *Purpose:* Hunter Hare Quail Pointer Retriever	50-60 lbs. 20-24 inch	++ ***	Elbow Dysplasia Hip Dysplasia	Mesomorphic	Hunting Pointing Retrieving 'Swimming' Tracking Watch Dog Jog - Great	Reserved with strangers, energetic, gentle, devoted, friendly, can be high strung, good hunting dog, eager to please, excitable, great swimmer *Working Dog:* Needs to have a job to do to keep mentally and physically stimulated

CANINE SPORTS/ACTIVITIES

There is a wide variety of canine/human sports to choose from, but there are also many things to consider before making that choice. The first thing to think about is the purpose: fun, exercise or competition? If you already own a dog, you want to find an activity that fits BOTH of you. You may think, well I am just going to get my dog into Flyball, so why worry about me. YOU have to have the patience and skill to teach him.

If you are looking to get a puppy and your goals are competition, I have suggested some 'breed types' for each activity or sports that are breed specific. For example, you may have a border collie that loves to chase, but the AKC will only allow certain sight hounds to participate in lure coursing. On the other hand, a corgi may not be the best choice for agility, but that doesn't mean he won't win. Looking at breed types does not mean they will be sure winners, or even enjoy the sport, but it may give you some insight.

As mentioned previously, two things to look at are 'what the canine was bred to do' and 'body type' (ecto, endo, meso, etc) This is very important when you are picking out a mixed breed puppy, especially if you are not sure what the mix is. If you are picking a puppy at a shelter and you have no history of the parents, spend some time playing with the puppy to see what kind of instincts they have. I had a dog in the past that was an Airedale terrier/lab mix. When we got her, she had very short hair and looked like a lab with short black hair with white patches. After several months, we had a long-legged lab with longish/curly/wiry, reddish/black hair, and the personality of a terrier. The dog I have pictured on the rocker board is a lab/Rottweiler mix. He has the look of a Rottweiler and the personality of a lab (loves to swim and not a great guard dog). In other words, even when you know the mix, you do not know which side will be more dominant.

Canine Sports are split up into several sections, which may or may not include:

- Precautions: There is a general precaution section below and sport specific precautions throughout.

- Sport

- Breed type and/or Body type: This is only a suggestion of type breed MAY excel in this sport if you are competing. This does not mean that other breeds will not succeed. See **Body Type** for more information.

    o Ecotomorphic: Tall, Long Limb, Light boned.

    o Mesomorphic: Medium Build , Moderate boned, Well muscled

    o Endomorphic: Average/Large size, Heavy Boned

    o Achondroplastic Dwarf: Relatively normal bodies (may be slightly elongated) Short legs

    o Pituitary Dwarf: Small, but relatively equal body/leg size

    o Giants: Larger size. Can be ecto., meso., or endo.

- Training: This is NOT a skills training book, but may give some suggestions or where to find information.

- Commands: Common commands on some sport.

- Equipment: Suggested equipment needed for sports.

- References or great books/websites.

Please see Individual Sections for References and Specific Precautions for that particular Sport/Activity

General Precautions:

- If you are new to the sport, make sure you and your dog get approval by your individual medical professionals as needed (veterinarian or MD)

- Make sure you warm up and cool down as appropriate. A nice walk prior to starting will warm up the muscles. (See the 3rd book in the series on Canine and Human Conditioning)

- If you are training a puppy, make sure they are 12-18 months old before doing any heavy work, depending on the breed.

- If you and/or your canine companion are 'out of shape', please start slow.

- Watch the 'gait pattern' or the way the dog walks before starting. He should have a smooth gait without limping. If you notice any discrepancies in gait before or after starting your sport, check with your vet to make sure there is no arthritis, hip dysplasia or other physical abnormality.

- Your dog should know basic commands before trying to teach sport specific commands, such as NO, SIT, STAY and COME.

- Like any sport, on hot humid days, it is best to work in the evening and early morning to avoid overheating. Provide plenty of water for both you and your dog. Be aware that arctic and brachycephalic (short nosed) breeds need to be watched closely in the hot weather. Humans also need to be careful to watch for heat related symptoms as well.

- Cold weather may be great for arctic type breeds, but humans should dress appropriately, preferably in layers. It is just as important to hydrate properly in winter months.

- Depending on the type of terrain, dog booties may be needed. This will protect the canines' paws in cold weather preventing ice from accumulating between the pads. It will also protect their paws on rough terrain.

Although many websites will tell you any dog can participate, please be aware of what the dog was bred to do, especially mixed breeds.

DOG and HUMAN SPORTS
Quick Summary & Precautions

Canicross
- Running – being pulled by your dog

Rollerjoring
- Skating – being pulled by your dog

Skijoring
- Cross country skiing - being pulled by your dog

Bikejoring
- Bike riding – being pulled by your dog, although can go by your side

Dog Scootering
- Scooter – being pulled by your dog

General Precautions:
- If you are new to the sport, make sure you and your dog get approval by your individual medical professionals as needed (veterinarian or MD)
- Make sure you warm up and cool down as appropriate. A nice walk prior to starting will warm up the muscles. (See the 3rd book in the series on Canine and Human Conditioning)
- If you are training a puppy, make sure they are 12-18 months old before doing any heavy work, depending on the breed.
- If you and/or your canine companion are 'out of shape', please start slow.
- Watch the 'gait pattern' or the way the dog walks before starting. He should have a smooth gait without limping. If you notice any discrepancies in gait before or after starting your sport, check with your vet to make sure there is no arthritis, hip dysplasia or other physical abnormality.
- Your dog should know basic commands before trying to teach sport specific commands, such as NO, SIT, STAY and COME.
- Like any sport, on hot humid days, it is best to work in the evening and early morning to avoid overheating. Provide plenty of water for both you and your dog. Be aware that arctic and brachycephalic (short nosed) breeds need to be watched closely in the hot weather. Humans also need to be careful to watch for heat related symptoms as well.
- Cold weather may be great for arctic type breeds, but humans should dress appropriately, preferably in layers. It is just as important to hydrate properly in winter months.
- Depending on the type of terrain, dog booties may be needed. This will protect the canines' paws in cold weather preventing ice from accumulating between the pads. It will also protect their paws on rough terrain.

Although many websites will tell you any dog can participate, please be aware of what the dog was bred to do, especially mixed breeds.

Precautions

- See General Precautions.
- **Dogs should be at least 30 lbs. (try a scooter if you have a smaller dog)**
- This book is not on skills training, so if you are going to try canicross, make sure YOU can run first.
- Depending on the type of terrain, dog booties may be needed. This will protect the canines feet in cold weather preventing ice from accumulating between the pads. It will also protect their feet on rough terrain.
- Running on asphalt can be harsh on both you and your dog. The dog pulling you can put extra stress on your ankles, hips and knees. (and possibly your back if you do not have the belt attached properly) This can also wear down the pads of the dog's feet.
- For the following sports, start your training with ONE dog if you are new to the event.
-
- For newbie's, it is advisable to start with Canicross and then work up to the other sports in this section. People who have experience with mushing and skijoring may find canicross more difficult because THEY have to keep up with their dog, especially if you have a fast dog or are training with more than one.

CANICROSS - *Running with your Dog*	
BREED TYPE and/or BODY TYPE	Mesomorphic (over 30 lbs.) or Ectomorphic (Caution: sight hounds may bolt after prey, and may not do well with long distance running).
DESCRIPTION	In canicross, you are not simply running with your dog, you are being pulled. • Canicross has its benefits over running with the dog by your side because you are attached to the dog in front of you by a tow line that is connected to a waist belt that you wear. This leaves your hands free and prevents disruption of your body's natural rhythm with arm swing and trunk rotation. • If you have a dog that likes to pull, this may also prevent sore shoulders, arms and back. • Some people also use poles which are beneficial in increasing upper body strength, and keep the muscles toned for those who participate in skijoring in the winter. • Most humans run at a speed for about 6-10 miles per hour, where an average speed of a dog is around 25 miles per hour. Jogging in humans is defined as running less than an 8-minute mile. *"You are only as fast as your slowest dog",* **which in Canicross means YOU (unless your participating with a small dog).**
PRECAUTIONS	• See General Precautions. • **Dogs should be at least 30 lbs. (try a scooter if you have a smaller dog)** • This book is not on skills training, so if you are going to try canicross, make sure YOU can run first. • Depending on the type of terrain, dog booties may be needed. This will protect the canines feet in cold weather preventing ice from accumulating between the pads. It will also protect their feet on rough terrain. • Running on asphalt can be harsh on both you and your dog. The dog pulling you can put extra stress on your ankles, hips and knees. (and possibly your back if you do not have the belt attached properly) This can also wear down the pads of the dog's feet. • For the following sports, start your training with ONE dog if you are new to the event. • For newbie's, it is advisable to start with Canicross and then work up to the other sports in this section. People who have experience with mushing and skijoring may find canicross more difficult because THEY have to keep up with their dog, especially if you have a fast dog or are training with more than one.
TRAINING **Human**	YOU must be in shape before trying to run with your dog. Like any sport, you may need to practice the skill by yourself before introducing your canine into the sport. If you already have experience with running, *skip this section.* If not, here are some tips. • Alternate walking and jogging in about 50-yard intervals. Try to start out on fairly flat ground at the beginning and gradually work up to inclines. Repeat these intervals 10-20 times. • You can gradually increase the intervals and distance. If your eventual goal is to race, find out the average racing distance needed. • When you feel YOU can comfortably fast walk / jog at least a mile, you can introduce your canine companion to the sport. Any shorter length on your part may confuse the dog with you having to stop and start again constantly. (See Canine training below) • Increase stride frequency and stride length to a comfortable running speed. • If you find the need to add weight, use a weighted vest. There is controversy as to whether holding weights in your hand can throw off your natural rhythm.

TRAINING **Canine**	As with you, if your dog has been a prior couch potato, don't try to run 2 miles on the first time out. • Besides road work (walking and jogging), if your dog likes to retrieve, this is a good way to get in shape. When retrieving, it is better to make sure the object has stopped or you can throw for distance before the dog gets to it. This will prevent the dog from jumping up and twisting his back or landing on his hind legs. • The next step is to find an incline, which is great for leg and core strengthening. As with any exercise, start with a low incline and gradually increase. When pulling, a dog is using different muscles then he is used to, so again, always start out slow and give the dog plenty of recovery time between outings. Here are some basics, but refer to the following websites for skills training: *https://skijorbikejorcanicross.blogspot.com/2008/05/training-lead-dogpart1.html* or *https://www.skijor.com/* • First of all, the dog should be sociable and not aggressive. • It is easier to train a dog that has NOT been taught to heel, as the dog will need to pull in front of you. • Start by having the dog get used to the harness. He should eventually relate the harness with pulling and the leash with walking. • Hook up to the dog. You may want to just hold the tow line at the beginning. Have someone get in front of the dog with him a stay position. The other person can then call the dog forward. Praise the dog if he stays in front and starts to pull. Increase the distance each time until he understands the command (see commands below). • When you are eventually running with the dog, start with low mileage and practice on a trail with little distractions. • Always make sure you have plenty of water for both of you, as well as a baggy for picking up waste.
COMMANDS	Make sure your dog is proficient at these commands before taking him on a trail where there will be other people or dogs. • **LINE OUT**: The line should be taut with the dog in front of you. Make sure when you teach this command you are consistent. • **HIKE**: Go • **GEE**: Turn Right. Pull the line to the right for training. DO NOT jerk the line. • **HA** or **HAW**: Turn Left. Pull the line to the left for training. DO NOT jerk the line. • **GEE OVER**: Stay to the right. • **HAW OVER**: Stay to the left. • **STRAIGHT**: Keep going straight if there is more than one trail. • **ON BY:** This is used to pass other runners or to avoid distractions. • **COME AROUND**: U-Turn. • **WHOA**: Stop. Tug on the harness or You stop. • **EASY**: Slow down.

EQUIPMENT	A great book I found on equipment and skijoring/canicross is *Ski Spot Run* by **Haakenstad and Thompson**
	
	• **Harness**
	The *X-back harness* is preferred.
	  o It is extremely important that the harness be fitted properly and must conform to the dogs body type.
	  o No moving part on the dog should hit the harness. A misaligned harness can cause musculoskeletal problems, as well as chaffing in short haired dogs.
	  o You can also get padding for the neck and chest.
	  o If you're not sure, find someone in your area that specializes in fitting dogs for harnesses, as this is the most important piece of equipment you will purchase.

- **Towline and Shock Cord**
  The towline is the connection between you and your dog.
  - The best type of towline is made from polyethylene. You may also want to invest in arctic-grade if you plan on using the line for skijoring in the winter months.
  - The only difference between the line for skijoring and canicross is that the skijoring line is longer, usually about 9 1/2 feet for one dog, 11 for two dogs and 12 for 3, where the canicross is about 6-7 feet for one dog.
  - You will also need a shock cord or bungee cord to protect from hard jolts that acts as a shock absorber between dog and human.
  - If you run more than one dog get another line with a longer bungee section.
  - A small brass swivel snap attaches the line to the dog's harness.
  - Stronger materials are stainless steel or solid bronze.
    (If running more than one dog, see Neck Line in Skijoring section below)

- **Belt**
  The waist belt is worn by the human.
  - The most common belt is the 4".
  - There are different opinions on where the belt should be in terms of center of gravity. Some say wear it at the center of gravity and others say above the waist offers more "adjustment options for countering pulling forces" (*Ski Spot Run, Thompson and Haakenstad, p 101*)
  - There are others that say the ones that wrap your butt and pulls you at a lower center of gravity is better. *http://skijorbikejorcanicross.blogspot.com/2008/05/equipment-needed-for-skijoring.html* .
  - Most of these books and sites are concentrating on skijoring and not canicross. If you don't have a professional shop to fit you in your area, just experiment to find which better fits you.
  - A quick release or panic snap will be needed in case you need to disengage from the dog immediately.
  - Make sure the snap remains with the belt when it is released so it stays with you instead of dragging behind the dog.
  - You can also get removable leg straps that can be used if you choose to also do skijoring in the winter.

Once you and your dog have canicross down, you can move on to skijoring in the winter or rollerjoring, bikejoring or scootering in the other months.

ROLLERJORING – *Rollerblading or Skating with your Dog*	
BREED TYPE and/or BODY TYPE	Mesomorphic (over 30 lbs.) or Ectomorphic (Caution: sight hounds may bolt after prey and may not do well with long distance running).
DESCRIPTION	Make sure you and your dog are proficient in canicross before adding skates. • This sport does require that you have training in inline skating or roller skis, and that your dog knows his commands. • This sport is more dangerous because you need to have control at a higher speed. You need to be able to stop immediately.
PRECAUTIONS	See General Precautions and Precautions above in addition to following: • Stay out of high traffic areas. Try to stay on walking trails that have little pedestrian traffic as well. • Use a helmet and protective gear. • At the beginning, do not attach your dog to your canicross/skijoring belt. This way you can let go of the lead until you are completely comfortable with you and your dog's performance. • This book is not on skills training, so if you are going to try rollerblading or skating make sure YOU can skate before introducing your dog into the mix. • Do not use more than one dog for this sport. • Practice stopping, as well as practice an emergency stop in case the situation calls for it. Aim for a soft place to land if you must go to the ground quickly to stop. Because of the speed, keep in mind there is less time to react if the situation calls for it compared to canicross. • In roller-skiing you will need to use your belt to keep your hands free to use the ski poles, so make sure you are proficient in rollerblading with your dog first.
TRAINING **Human**	This is not a lesson in rollerblading, so make sure before you start, you are proficient without your dog and can stop, turn and have control over your speed. • Use a regular leash or hold the bungee lead before trying to attach it to the skijoring belt. Once you and your companion are comfortable, you can progress to attaching the lead to the belt. • You may want to practice with another human taking the dogs place at the beginning. Although your friend may not run as fast, it will give you a feel for sudden turns, braking and slowing down before attaching the dog. • Try practicing over several different terrains and areas without the dog first. Become familiar with the paths you are going to take.

TRAINING
 	
Canine
	Practice the commands that you learned in canicross above.
	
	• A command that you may want to go over again is the "easy" command for slowing down. This will be necessary on declines.
	  o Say 'Easy' while applying the brakes at the same time to give him the signal to slow down.
	  o Practice this on a level area before you get to the point of going downhill.
	• Make sure your dog understands the stay command before you hook yourself up. You do not want to start when the dog is excited and unable to control himself, as he will start before you are ready.
	  o You may also want to have someone else hold the dog until you say 'hike'.
	• Keep your eye on the towline.
	  o Brake when the dog slows to prevent slacking in the towline, which can tangle in the dogs legs or get under the wheels and cause you to fall.

COMMANDS	Make sure your dog is proficient at these commands before taking him on a trail where there will be other people or dogs. • **LINE OUT**: The line should be taut with the dog in front of you. Make sure when you teach this command you are consistent. • **HIKE**: Go • **GEE**: Turn Right. Pull the line to the right for training. DO NOT jerk the line. • **HA** or **HAW**: Turn Left. Pull the line to the left for training. DO NOT jerk the line. • **GEE OVER**: Stay to the right. • **HAW OVER**: Stay to the left. • **STRAIGHT**: Keep going straight if there is more than one trail. • **ON BY:** This is used to pass other runners or to avoid distractions. • **COME AROUND**: U-Turn. • **WHOA**: Stop. Tug on the harness or You stop. • **EASY**: Slow down.
EQUIPMENT	• **Harness, Towline and Belt** as above in Canicross.  • **Protective gear** This is a must!!! A helmet, wrist guards, knee guards, elbow guards and even tailbone guards are available. • **Towline** As compared to canicross, the line for rollerjoring is about 9 1/2 feet. • **Tow rope handle** If you do not feel comfortable attaching your dog to your belt, try getting a tow rope handle that can be dropped in case of emergency. This is advisable for the beginner or people who have unpredictable dogs. The downside of this is that it does not provide proper form on your part with decreased trunk rotation and arm swing. • **Skates** Unless you are sure that you will *only* be skating on pavement, get off-road rollerblades or roller-skis that you can use on paths that may have dirt or gravel. • **Poles** If you are planning on skijoring during the winter months, you can use ski poles. Of course, this will require that you do not have to use the tow rope handle.

SKIJORING – *Skiing with your Dog*	
BREED TYPE and/or BODY TYPE	Mesomorphic (over 30 lbs.) and breeds that can endure cold weather.
DESCRIPTION	Now that you have canicross down, let's add skis to the mix. • As mentioned before, know how to cross country ski by yourself before adding your dog to the line. • See the website *https://www.skijor.com/* for instructions.
PRECAUTIONS	See General Precautions and *Precautions* above in addition to following: • If you *do not* have an arctic type breed, or *do* have a short haired breed, you may need to add a 'coat'. See Equipment below. • As with rollerjoring, at the beginning, you may want to use a tow rope handle until you get used to skiing with your pet. • This is not a book on skills training, so if you are going to try skijoring make sure YOU can ski before introducing your dog into the mix. • Start with one dog before adding more - no more than 3. • Be very careful not to run into your dog. • Pay attention to the surface you are skiing on and look ahead at the area: 　○ Shallow snow: It may be hard to stop or slow down. 　○ Areas or patches with no snow: You may stop abruptly. 　○ Ice: A hazard in itself. If it has thawed and frozen over repeatedly, make sure your dog is wearing booties to prevent cuts on the pads of his feet. 　○ Avoid areas with sharp turns.
TRAINING **Human**	This is not a lesson in skijoring so make sure before you start, you are proficient *without* your dog. Practice your turns and stops ahead of time. • Balance: Make sure you have good balance. Practice going around sharp corners. Make yourself an obstacle course in all types of terrain. 　○ A dog can run faster than you can ski uphill, so practice inclines and declines as well. (Do all this without the dog first). • If the dog lunges forward, assume the ski tuck position. This will stabilize your back/hips to help prevent back injuries. • You may not want to use your poles at the beginning.
TRAINING **Canine**	Make sure the dog is proficient in canicross, as well as the commands. • A command that you may want to go over again is the "easy" command for slowing down. 　○ This will be necessary on inclines where your dog can run faster than you. • Make sure your dog understands the 'line out' command before starting. 　○ This is important to keep the line taught before starting. • Keep the beginning sessions short. Vary the run distance each day. If your dog is not as enthusiastic, take several days off and do something else for fun.

COMMANDS	Make sure your dog is proficient at these commands before taking him on a trail where there will be other people or dogs. • **LINE OUT**: The line should be taut with the dog in front of you. Make sure when you teach this command you are consistent. • **HIKE**: Go • **GEE**: Turn Right. Pull the line to the right for training. DO NOT jerk the line. • **HA** or **HAW**: Turn Left. Pull the line to the left for training. DO NOT jerk the line. • **GEE OVER**: Stay to the right. • **HAW OVER**: Stay to the left. • **STRAIGHT**: Keep going straight if there is more than one trail. • **ON BY:** This is used to pass other runners or to avoid distractions.  • **COME AROUND**: U-Turn. • **WHOA**: Stop. Tug on the harness or You stop. • **EASY**: Slow down.

EQUIPMENT	• **Harness, Towline** and **Belt** as above in Canicross.
	 • **Towline**
	 The towline for skijoring is about 9 1/2 feet for one dog, 11 feet for two dogs and 12 feet for 3.
	 • **Tow rope handle**
	 If you do not feel comfortable attaching your dog to your belt at the beginning, try getting a tow rope handle that can be dropped in case of emergency.
	 • **Helmet**
	 Use a helmet if you are going on rough terrain that has a lot of turns and trees.
	 • **Eyewear**
	 Protective eyewear is necessary to guard the eyes from debris kicked up from the running dogs, as well as shield them from glare off the snow.
	     ○ Make sure they provide access to peripheral vision, as well as being shatter proof.
	     ○ If you are skiing at night, you may need a second pair that is not tinted.
	 • **Skies and poles**
	 Cross country skis are preferably *without* metal edges that can cause injury to the dog.
	 • **Neckline**
	 Only needed when working two dogs side by side. Connects two dogs together.
	     ○ The collars it attaches to should be the same size as the harness you are using.
	     ○ Make sure the collars are snug (about two finger widths) so it doesn't pull off.
	     ○ You can also run the dogs one in back of the other without the neckline.
	 • **Jacket**
	 Dress accordingly depending on the weather.
	     ○ This also goes for your dog. If you have a short haired dog, make sure the jacket you get is waterproof/resistant and provides free movement of all joints.

BIKEJORING – *Biking with your Dog*	
BREED TYPE and/or BODY TYPE	Mesomorphic (over 30 lbs.) or Ectomorphic (Caution: sight hounds may bolt after prey and may not do well with long distance running).
DESCRIPTION	Very simply, your dog is pulling you while you are on a bike. • The downfall of this is that bikejoring is more exercise for your dog than you, unless you are going up a lot of hills that require you to peddle more often. • You can also try biking on sandy or grassy surfaces that provide more resistance. • See the website *https://www.skijor.com/* for more instructions and detailed equipment needs.
PRECAUTIONS	See General Precautions and *Precautions* above in addition to following: • You may want to start by not attaching the line to the bike at the beginning. o Hold the line - **do not wrap it around your hand**. • This book is not on skills training, so if you are going to try bikejoring make sure YOU know how to ride a bike before introducing your dog into the mix. • Start with one dog before adding more - no more than 3. • Be very careful not to run into your dog. • If you choose to do a lot of biking on asphalt, invest in some dog booties for protection. • Decide if your dog is a front runner and can pull. If not, you may need a side mount attachment. *See equipment below.*

TRAINING
 	
Human
	• This is not a lesson in biking so make sure before you start, you are proficient *without* your dog . Practice your turns and stops ahead of time. Also make sure you find as website or book as above on the proper way to attach the towline to the bike.
	• Do NOT wear a skijoring belt.
	   o The towline gets connected to the base of the handlebars or Springer attachment (see equipment below and check out the website *https://www.skijor.com/* for proper attachment of equipment)
	• Practice 'feathering' your brakes. If you are biking on asphalt (not recommended for canine's pads), you may need to keep a constant pace.
	• In this sport YOU have to be in complete control, especially of your speed.
	   o Practice this not only on straight runs, but also on downhill sharp turns.
	   o Know what speed limit works for you before hooking up your dog.
	• Start out with a friend pulling you instead of a dog.
	   o Practice different trails, inclines, declines and feathering the brakes.
	   o If you are using a Springer on the side, try seeing what it is like turning with your friend next to you in both directions.
	   o If running in front, have them pull you abruptly from side to side and pull from the front. In other words, try being pulled in every direction that your dog would pull you in so you can get a feel for any adjustments you will need to make when you finally have your canine attached.

TRAINING **Canine**	Practice the commands and training that you learned in canicross above. A command that you may want to go over again is the "easy" command for slowing down. This will be necessary on declines and sharp turns. • Keep the beginning sessions short. Vary the run distance each day. • If your dog is not as enthusiastic, take several days off and do something else for fun.

COMMANDS	Make sure your dog is proficient at these commands before taking him on a trail where there will be other people or dogs. • **LINE OUT**: The line should be taut with the dog in front of you. Make sure when you teach this command you are consistent. • **HIKE**: Go • **GEE**: Turn Right. Pull the line to the right for training. DO NOT jerk the line. • **HA** or **HAW**: Turn Left. Pull the line to the left for training. DO NOT jerk the line. • **GEE OVER**: Stay to the right. • **HAW OVER**: Stay to the left. • **STRAIGHT**: Keep going straight if there is more than one trail. • **ON BY:** This is used to pass other runners or to avoid distractions. • **COME AROUND**: U-Turn. • **WHOA**: Stop. Tug on the harness or You stop. • **EASY**: Slow down.

EQUIPMENT	See *https://www.skijor.com/* for a detailed description of equipment.
	
	• **Mountain Bike**
	Good quality mountain bike
	• **Knobby tires**
	Good traction is needed
	• **Excellent brakes**
	It is important to go to a bike shop and get brakes that will work for the terrain where you will be biking 
	• **Front end suspension or duel suspension**
	• **Fenders**
	• **Springer attachment**
	A Springer keeps the dog at the side of the bicycle if your dog is not a front runner.
	   ○ A shorter lead also attaches to the Springer.
	   ○ You will need a wider trail to ride on since the dog is beside you and not in front.
	   ○ This may also confuse the dog if you run with your dog with him in the front and bike with him in a heel position on the side.
	• **Bungee towline** - See Skijoring
	• **X Back Harness** - See Canicross
	• **Eye protection** - See Skijoring
	• **Helmet.**

SCOOTERING – *Scooter with your Dog*	
BREED TYPE and/or BODY TYPE	The great thing about dog scootering is that not only do you have a bit more control that bikejoring, but you can do this with smaller dogs.
DESCRIPTION	Very simply, your dog is pulling you while you are on a bike. • The downfall of this is that bikejoring is more exercise for your dog than you, unless you are going up a lot of hills that require you to peddle more often. • You can also try biking on sandy or grassy surfaces that provide more resistance. • See the website *https://www.skijor.com/* for more instructions and detailed equipment needs.
PRECAUTIONS	See General Precautions and *Precautions* above in addition to following: • You may consider bikejoring if you plan to go up a lot of steep hills. Scooters are made for a flatter surface. • Start with one dog before adding more - no more than 2. • Be very careful not to run into your dog.

TRAINING
 	
Human
	This is not a lesson in biking so make sure before you start, you are proficient *without* your dog. Practice your turns and stops ahead of time.
	• You can help the dogs a bit more by using your foot to kick or running with the scooter, so it is not all on the dog.
	  ○ On the other hand, this can also be distracting to the dog. This can also cause slack in the line when the dog is pulling.
	• As mentioned in precautions, this is not a sport if you have a lot of steep inclines to go up.
	  ○ This may require you to run with the scooter when necessary.

TRAINING **Canine**	• Practice the commands and training that you learned in canicross and bikejoring above. • Keep the beginning sessions short. Vary the run distance each day. • If your dog is not as enthusiastic, take several days off and do something else for fun.
COMMANDS	Make sure your dog is proficient at these commands before taking him on a trail where there will be other people or dogs. • **LINE OUT**: The line should be taut with the dog in front of you. Make sure when you teach this command you are consistent. • **HIKE**: Go • **GEE**: Turn Right. Pull the line to the right for training. DO NOT jerk the line. • **HA** or **HAW**: Turn Left. Pull the line to the left for training. DO NOT jerk the line. • **GEE OVER**: Stay to the right. • **HAW OVER**: Stay to the left. • **STRAIGHT**: Keep going straight if there is more than one trail. • **ON BY:** This is used to pass other runners or to avoid distractions. • **COME AROUND**: U-Turn. • **WHOA**: Stop. Tug on the harness or You stop. • **EASY**: Slow down.
EQUIPMENT	See Bikejoring for most equipment, except scooter. • **Scooter:** Off road version with good quality brakes. Weight should be approximately that of a mountain bike.

References

Active Dog Sports - *Articles on Canicross, Bikejoring, Scootering, Skijoring, etc.*
https://activedogsports.com/category/dog-mushing/

American Kennel Club – *How to get Started in Canicross* - https://www.akc.org/expert-advice/health/canicross-goes-beyond-running-with-dogs/

Canicross by Mike Callahan. Previously published in Mushing Magazine November/December 2001
http://www.skijor.com/canicross.html

Canicross USA - https://canicrossusa.org/

Doggie Sport - *Skijoring With Dogs | Getting Started, Equipment & Breeds!* by Sacha Parent
https://doggiesport.com/skijoring-with-dogs/

KUHL - *Feel the Pull: Dog Skijoring and Urban Mushing* - https://www.kuhl.com/borninthemountains/dog-skijoring

MUSH! *A Beginner's Manual of Sled Dog Training,* by LaBelle, Charlene - editor for Sierra Nevada Dog Drivers, Inc.

NEEWA - *What Is Bikejoring? The Ultimate Guide To Dog Bikejoring* -
https://www.neewadogs.com/pages/bikejoring

North American Canicross - https://nacanicross.com/

Rover.com (The Dog People) - *Skijoring is the Best Dog Sport You've Never Heard Of*
https://www.rover.com/blog/skijoring-dog-sport-skis/

Running Dogs (blog) http://skijorbikejorcanicross.blogspot.com/2008/05/equipment-needed-for-skijoring.html

Sled Dog Central http://www.sleddogcentral.com/skijorarticles.htm#introduction

Ski Spot Run by Haakenstad and Thompson for lots of information on skijoring and more.

SkiJor Now http://www.skijornow.com

DOG PULLING SPORTS
Quick Summary & Precautions

Weight Pulling
- Weight pulling competitions were originally designed for sled dog breeds. Now it has expanded to not only the bull breeds, but most breeds can participate, even if they are less than 30 lbs.

Carting/Sulky
- Unlike weight pulling, Carting or Draft Work is pulling a wheeled vehicle, and can be with a 'driver' (human) in the cart controlling the cart, wagon or sulky.

Mushing
- Mushing is a general term for a sport or transport method powered by dogs, and includes carting, pulka, scootering, sled dog racing, skijoring, freighting, and weight pulling.

Sledding
- Sledding can be done with as little as one dog, although to compete, the minimum is 3 depending on the competition.

Sled Dog Racing
- Sled Dog Racing is a winter sport that is a timed competition which uses a team of dogs to pull a driver that stands on a runner.

Pulka or Nordic Style Dog Mushing
- Pulka integrates dogs, a sled, and a skier. Pulka can be done with one dog or multiple dogs, depending on the amount of weight being pulled. In addition to being a competitive sport, is also used by some winter adventurers to move supplies.

General Precautions:
- If you are new to the sport, make sure you and your dog get approval by your individual medical professionals as needed (veterinarian or MD)
- Make sure you warm up and cool down as appropriate. A nice walk prior to starting will warm up the muscles. (See the 3rd book in the series on Canine and Human Conditioning)
- If you are training a puppy, make sure they are 12-18 months old before doing any heavy work, depending on the breed.
- If you and/or your canine companion are 'out of shape', please start slow.
- Watch the 'gait pattern' or the way the dog walks before starting. He should have a smooth gait without limping. If you notice any discrepancies in gait before or after starting your sport, check with your vet to make sure there is no arthritis, hip dysplasia or other physical abnormality.
- Your dog should know basic commands before trying to teach sport specific commands, such as NO, SIT, STAY and COME.
- Like any sport, on hot humid days, it is best to work in the evening and early morning to avoid overheating. Provide plenty of water for both you and your dog. Be aware that arctic and brachycephalic (short nosed) breeds need to be watched closely in the hot weather. Humans also need to be careful to watch for heat related symptoms as well.
- Cold weather may be great for arctic type breeds, but humans should dress appropriately, preferably in layers. It is just as important to hydrate properly in winter months.
- Depending on the type of terrain, dog booties may be needed. This will protect the canines' paws in cold weather preventing ice from accumulating between the pads. It will also protect their paws on rough terrain.

Although many websites will tell you any dog can participate, please be aware of what the dog was bred to do, especially mixed breeds.

Precautions

- See General Precautions
- If you are new to the sport, make sure your dog gets approval by a veterinarian.
  - Any dog with hip dysplasia, slipped stifle, patella luxation or any arthritic conditions should not participate in any weight pulling type of activities, as this will only exacerbate their condition.
  - Any dog showing any type of discomfort should not be allowed to pull weight, cart, or hike.
- Make sure your dog warms up and cools downs as appropriate. A nice walk prior to starting will warm up the muscles.
- Puppies/dogs should be well socialized, especially bully breeds that may more often be seen in the weight pulling competitions.
  - Take your puppy or dog to many different environments and introduce them to the many sounds they will hear if your goal is to eventually compete in any of the sports listed.

WEIGHT PULLING	
BREED TYPE and/or BODY TYPE	Endomorphic/bull breeds.
DESCRIPTION	Weight pulling competitions were originally designed for sled dog breeds. Now it has expanded to not only the bull breeds, but most breeds can participate, even if they are less than 30 lbs. • There are different weight classes, so any size dog is welcome in the competition, although *I believe* there are some breeds, such as the Italian Greyhound, that are not made to pull weight due to their fragile bones. • There are several competitions with different rules, but for the most part there is a rail pull, a wheeled cart pull or a sled pull on snow for about 16 feet. • An example of the rules can be found on the **Tri State Alaskan Malamute Club** *http://www.tsamc.org/forms/Rules.html* **or The International Weight Pull Association** *http://www.iwpa.net/Rules.html* . • Before starting, it is best to attend a weight pulling competition without your dog so that you can observe and talk to individuals that are competing.

WEIGHT PULLING COMPETITION RESTRICTIONS	• Dogs are not allowed if they are less than one year of age.
	   o They also need to be up to date on vaccines, and have proof of rabies vaccine.
	   o The dogs cannot be in heat or pregnant and cannot be considered to be vicious (which is always based on individual dog and not breed characteristics or reputation).
	• Dogs will not be allowed if they show signs of aggression towards the handler, judge, any person or other dogs.
	• Abuse of the dog will not be tolerated.
	• If the dog cannot complete the pull, a 'no-pull' will be assigned, although the dog will be allowed to finish with less weight for his 'ego'.

TRAINING	▪ No heavy weight training should begin until most dogs are 1 1/2 to 2 years old, especially larger breeds.
	   o Puppies need time for their bones to grow properly.
	   o A puppy that is pushed too hard at a young age will have a very short run at this sport and will cause joint problems at a young age.
	   o A dog that is trained at two years and older has more of a chance to continue this sport until they are 10-12 years old, as opposed to a retirement age of 3 with early training.
	▪ You can start your puppy early with introducing the harness and basic commands.
	   o You can also have them pull light objects to get used to the feel and sounds of something dragging behind them.
	▪ Getting used to the harness may be different for each dog.
	   o If you originally trained your dog walking with a harness instead of a collar, this should be easy for you. For others, take it slow.
	   o First let them smell the harness and play with it so they do not fear the object. The first time you put it on, make sure you associate it with something pleasant, like food or playing with them to distract them.
	   o Only have them wear it for short periods of time, and then take it off, eventually increasing the time.
	   o DO NOT make a big deal or baby the dog while wearing it, as you will just encourage fear.

TRAINING
 	
Continued
	▪ Depending on the age and the size of the dog, once the dog is used to the harness attach a water jug for them to pull, eventually adding coins or gravel to get them used to the noise when dragging the object.
	    o You may attach this by a long rope or cloths line, approximately 15-20 so they are not too spooked at the beginning.
	
	▪ COMMANDS: The basic command you will give to your dog is 'pull', 'work' or 'come' - it can also be a hand signal, like touching your finger to the ground.
	▪ You can either stand in front of the dog (in competition, this would be at the finish line and call the dog).
	    o The other place is in the rear or side and 'drive' the dog forward.
	▪ It is best NOT to use food while training your puppy or dog, as this is not allowed in actual competition.
	    o Dogs have also been known to snap secondary to stress during competition when food is used as bait.
	▪ You can start your puppy off with an X back harness having him pull small objects, such as an empty children's sled, until he is mature enough to start actual pull training.
	▪ When your dog is mature enough to start training, most people will start by adding a foot or two of chain to the harness.
	    o To make it harder, have the dog go over grass, which will cause more resistance.
	    o You can then advance to a lightweight pull sled, and increase to a rubber tire.
	▪ Vary your training to every other day and change your pull distance frequently.
	    o Heavy short distances are better for building muscle mass.
	    o Lighter and longer distances build endurance.
	▪ Core training, balance, endurance training with running and strength training should all be incorporated into your dog's fitness routine.
	▪ The biggest advice is to make it fun. Give plenty of praise.
	    o If you reduce your dog's confidence, chances are he will not pull for you.
	    o This is not a sport that requires heavy handed training.
	    o Stop your training sessions while your dog is still having fun *before* he gets too tired or bored.
	▪ If your dog is going to compete, it may be beneficial to practice pulling bags of dog food. Some companies sponsor the events and have the dogs pull bags of dry dog food, which may be a part of the prize to the winner.
	    o Have the dog practice with this ahead of time so that they will not be distracted by the smell if they enter a competition with food used as the weight.

EQUIPMENT	• **Harness**
	Freight harness. There are several types of harnesses available, including rolled, leather, and nylon.
	    o It is important that you do not get a racing harness, and that the front is highly padded.
	    o The harness should have room to be hooked up below the tail.
	    o If you have a dog with a thick coat, you may need more than one harness depending on the season.
	    o It is best to have the harness custom made to fit your dog.
	
	• **Spreader Bar**
	A spreader bar goes between the back sides of the harness.
	    o This is a dowel that holds the straps apart so the dog can extend his legs when pulling.
	
	• **Sled or cart to pull**
	This will really depend on what type of pulling you want to do.
	    o See appropriate organization for more info.

CARTING/SULKY

BREED TYPE and/or BODY TYPE	Endomorphic, Giant Breeds and Mesomorphic (over 35 lbs.). Other breeds can participate if not pulling people or heavy items in the cart (see below).
DESCRIPTION	Unlike weight pulling, Carting or Draft Work is pulling a wheeled vehicle, and can be with a 'driver' (human) in the cart controlling the cart, wagon or sulky. • Carts have two wheels; wagons have 4 wheels; sulky's can have two wheels with the driver standing. • You will follow the same basic instructions as weight pulling, but with carting, you are not adding weight. • You also will need to have your dog learn some basic commands, as they are not going in a straight line as with weight pulling competitions.

PRECAUTIONS	See General Precautions and *Precautions* above in addition to following:
	• Dogs should be over 35 lbs. if pulling a human.
	   ○ There are smaller carts for miniature dogs, but *obviously* you would not want to be driving the cart.
	• As with other dog sports, if you are traveling on pavement, you may look into booties for your dog to protect his paws.
	• Unlike weight pulling with bull breeds who arch their backs and 'dig in' for pulling short distances, dogs that pull carts over long distances should pull with a level top line (shoulder to tail should be flat along the spine) to prevent back injuries.
	   ○ Some sight hounds have normally arched backs and German Shepherds tend to have a sloping top line.
	• ***Be careful*** if you are using sight hounds to pull - not only are they anatomically not made to be pulling heavy weight, but they are also more apt bolt if they see a fuzzy little rabbit crossing the road.

TRAINING	**See Training** under Weight Pulling **above.** • If you are going to be pulling a driver, the total load of vehicle and driver should not weigh more than 3 times the dog's body weight. COMMANDS: • **GEE** - Turn Right • **HAW** - Turn Left • **BACK UP** - Back Cart Up • **START OR LET'S GO**- To Start Pulling Cart • **WHOA** –Stop • **STAY OR WAIT** - Dog Needs to Stay • **EASY** - Slow Down • **PULL** - Lean into the Pull Harder • **FASTER OR GO** - Speed Up • *Go to Dog and Human Sports for additional commands/training.* Start your training ***BEFORE*** getting into the cart. Make sure your canine friend has all the orders down before hitching up as well.

EQUIPMENT	• **Harness**
	This really depends on the type of vehicle you are going to pull or generally preference.
	  ○ *Parade Harness:* This harness has a padded strap across the chest, which attaches to straps or poles. This can be made of leather or nylon. The downside is that this type of harness can be constricting. OK for *light* loads.
	  ○ *Draft Harness:* Looks like a horse harness.
	  ○ *Siwash Harness:* Preferred. Similar to the Weight Pulling Harness without the spreader bar.
	    ▪ This harness leaves the shoulder assembly open to increase free range of motion of the front legs.
	
	• **Break Band**
	Attached to the harness and brake on the cart to keep the cart coming forward and hitting the dog if they are going downhill or stopping fast
	
	• **Cart**
	This will really depend on the purpose for pulling.
	  ○ As above, there are 2 wheeled, 4 wheeled, Sulkies, and even a Travois, that has no wheels and is used mainly for dragging items over rough terrain.

MUSHING
Dry Land Mushing - See Carting, Bikejoring and Scootering for Training and Equipment

BREED TYPE and/or BODY TYPE	Mesomorphic (over 30 lbs.) and breeds that can endure cold weather.
DESCRIPTION	Excerpt from *http://en.wikipedia.org/wiki/Mushing:* '*Mushing is a general term for a sport or transport method powered by dogs, and includes carting, pulka, scootering, sled dog racing, skijoring, freighting, and weight pulling. More specifically, it implies the use of one or more dogs to pull a sled on snow.*  • *The term is thought to come from the French word marche, or go, run, the command to the team to commence pulling. "Mush!" is rarely used in modern parlance, however; "Hike!" is more common in English.* • *Mushing can be utilitarian, recreational, or competitive. Mushing as a sport is practiced worldwide, but primarily in North America and northern Europe. Racing associations such as the International Federation of Sleddog Sports (IFSS) and the International Sled Dog Racing Association (ISDRA) are working toward organizing the sport and in gaining Olympic recognition for mushing.* • *It is the state sport of Alaska.* • *Although dogsled racing gets more publicity and is seen now as the primary form of mushing, recreational mushing thrives as an unorganized sport providing healthy outdoor form of winter exercise for families.* • *Mushing for utilitarian purposes includes anything from hauling wood or delivering milk or the mail to rural travel and equipment hauling'.*

SLEDDING	
DESCRIPTION	Sledding can be done with as little as one dog, although to compete, the minimum is 3 depending on the competition. • See Carting for Training suggestions. • Several types of sleds can be used depending on what you are transporting (see equipment below). • This is a very expensive sport to compete in, but can be very rewarding for a hobby if you have 1-2 dogs that love to pull and enjoy the snow.

TEAM	If you decide to go into this sport to compete, here is what your pack will be made up of. 'Dog team members are given titles according to their position in the team relative to the sled.

	These include leaders or lead dogs, swing dogs, team dogs, and wheelers or wheel dogs.
	• **Lead dogs** steer the rest of the team and set the pace.
	• **Swing dogs** or point dogs are directly behind the leader (one dog if the team is in single hitch).
	   o They swing the rest of the team behind them in turns or curves on the trail. (Some mushers use the term swing dog to denote a team dog.)
	• **Team dogs** are those between the wheelers and the swing dogs, and add power to the team
	• **Wheel dogs** are those nearest the sled, and a good wheeler must have a relatively calm temperament so as not to be startled by the sled moving just behind it.
	   o Strength, steadiness, and ability to help guide the sled around tight curves are qualities valued in "wheelers."' *http://en.wikipedia.org/wiki/Mushing*
	
	Terminology from **The Official Site of The Iditarod** - *http://www.iditarod.com/learn/terminology.html*

EQUIPMENT	• **Sled**
	Generally a Basket type for shorter distances or Toboggans for longer distances over un-groomed trails.
	• **Harness**
	Siwash or X back Harness in Nylon material is the most popular. See *Carting* above. There is also an H-back harness that works well with distance mushers.
	• **Gangline**
	This is made up of several components, including the Towline, Tugline and Neckline (for more than one dog).
	   o These three lines are generally made from arctic-grade polyethylene and are used to attach the dogs to the sled.
	   o You will also need a shock cord or bungee cord to protect from hard jolts that acts as a shock absorber.
	• **Snow Hook**
	Anchor for the sled when it is stopped.
	• **Sled Bag**
	This is useful in carrying equipment.
	• **Snub Line**
	Line for securing the sled and team while you are stopped or hooking up other dogs.
	• **Booties** - As above in precautions.
	• **Coat**
	      Depending on the breed of the dog, a coat may be needed. Make sure YOU are wearing the proper snow gear as well.

SLED DOG RACING

BREED TYPE and/or BODY TYPE	Mesomorphic (over 30 lbs.) and breeds that can endure cold weather.
DESCRIPTION	Sled dog racing goes beyond the scope of this book. • Sled Dog Racing is a winter sport that is a timed competition which uses a team of dogs to pull a driver that stands on a runner. • Races can be relatively short sprints from 4>25 miles and as long as 200>1000 miles. • If this looks like something you would like be a part of, check out local clubs or attend some races to see what is involved. International Sled Dog Racing Association: ISDRA http://www.isdra.org The Official Site of The Iditarod - *http://www.iditarod.com/learn/terminology.html*

PULKA or NORDIC STYLE DOG MUSHING

BREED TYPE and/or BODY TYPE	Mesomorphic (over 30 lbs.) and breeds that can endure cold weather.

DESCRIPTION	*Definition by http://www.wisegeek.com/what-is-pulka.htm :*
	
	"Pulka is a type of winter sport popular in Scandinavia which has recently spread to other parts of the world. Pulka can be great fun and involves a high level of cooperation between people and animals for success.
	• *It integrates dogs, a sled, and a skier. Pulka can be done with one dog or multiple dogs, depending on the amount of weight being pulled.*
	• *In addition to being a competitive sport, is also used by some winter adventurers to move supplies.*
	• *Pulka begins with the dog or dogs, which are put into a harness attached to a small sled called a pulka.*
	• *In competition, the pulka is loaded with a set weight, which is around 40 pounds (20 kilograms) for male dogs and 33 pounds (15 kilograms) for females, who tend to be smaller and less able to bear heavy loads.*
	• *When used for recreation, the pulka may be left unloaded, or used for gear and supplies. The skier attaches him or herself to the pulka using a strap.*
	   o *Technically, the skier is not being pulled by the dogs, although flat terrain provides an opportunity to rest.*
	   o *The skier must work with the dogs to succeed, contributing on uphill climbs rather than acting as dead weight.*
	• *Pulka requires more coordination than traditional dog sledding, because in addition to handling the dogs, the skier must also stay upright and in control of his or her skis.*
	
	Pulka is most popular in Scandinavia and is not as well known in the United States where dog sledding and skijoring are more common winter sports with dogs.
	• *Pulka is recognized by the International Association of Sled Dog Sports as a sport, and competitions are regulated by that organization as well.*

EQUIPMENT	<ul><li>**Pulk (Small Sled)** The sled or Pulk is approximately 16 lbs. for a commercial grade. This can be pulled behind the skier instead of between the skier the canine.</li><li>**Shaft** "If the Pulk is being pulled behind the skijorer, a longer shaft needs to be attached, which are attached to a modified skijoring belt.<ul><li>When the pulk is between the skier and the dog, the dog is hooked to the pulk with ridged shafts.</li><li>When the skier is between the pulk and the dog, the ridged shafts for the pulk are attached to the skier. "*(MUSH! A Beginner's Manual of Sled Dog Training, by LaBelle, Charlene - editor)*</li></ul></li><li>**Skijoring Belt** (modified if needed), and other equipment listed in the Skijoring section.</li></ul>

References

American Kennel Club - *Tips on Doing Advanced Drafting Work With Your Dog*
https://www.akc.org/expert-advice/training/doing-advanced-drafting-work/

Carting with your Dog http://www.cartingwithyourdog.com/cfaq.html#Commands

Fun with Draft by Phil Chagnon https://bmdcc.ca/

Iditarod – Official Site http://www.iditarod.com/learn/terminology.html

International Weight Pull Association http://www.iwpa.net/Rules.html

MUSH! *A Beginner's Manual of Sled Dog Training,* by LaBelle, Charlene - editor for Sierra Nevada Dog Drivers, Inc.

Ski Spot Run by Haakenstad and Thompson for lots of information on skijoring and more.

Snowpaw Store https://snowpawstore.com/collections/weight-pull

Tri-State Alaskan Malamute Club http://www.tsamc.org/forms/Rules.html

Wikipedia: Drafting - https://en.wikipedia.org/wiki/Drafting_(dog)

Wikipedia: Sled Dog http://en.wikipedia.org/wiki/Sled_dogs

Wikipedia: Sled Dog Racing http://en.wikipedia.org/wiki/Sled_dog_racing .

What is Pulka? *By Wise Geek*   http://www.wisegeek.com/what-is-pulka.html

INSTINCT SPORTS
Quick Summary & Precautions

Earthdog
- Earthdog trials were set up for small short-legged terriers that were primarily bred to hunt vermin and other quarry that lives underground. Man made tunnels are set up for the dogs to negotiate following the scent of the rat or other quarry

Field Trials
- Field trials cover many hunting events, including retrieval, flushing and pointing. In field trials, dog and handler teams compete against one another, where there is only one winner in the end.

Retrieving
- Retrievers must remember where the bird went down, retrieve the bird from either land or water back to their handler.

Flushing
- These dogs must first hunt or find the prey and then flush it from its hiding place for the handler to shoot or capture.

Pointing
- Point out the game for the handler to shoot, and retrieve the downed bird to the handler.

Herding
- Whether you have a dog already that you would like to try herding with, or are looking to buy a herding dog, the first question you have to answer is what are you going to herd?

Tracking
Do you have a dog that loves to follow his nose? This may be the sport for you. Tracking, scent work or any general 'nose' work all require your dog to use his sense of smell.

General Precautions:
- If you are new to the sport, make sure you and your dog get approval by your individual medical professionals as needed (veterinarian or MD)
- Make sure you warm up and cool down as appropriate. A nice walk prior to starting will warm up the muscles. (See the 3rd book in the series on Canine and Human Conditioning)
- If you are training a puppy, make sure they are 12-18 months old before doing any heavy work, depending on the breed.
- If you and/or your canine companion are 'out of shape', please start slow.
- Watch the 'gait pattern' or the way the dog walks before starting. He should have a smooth gait without limping. If you notice any discrepancies in gait before or after starting your sport, check with your vet to make sure there is no arthritis, hip dysplasia or other physical abnormality.
- Your dog should know basic commands before trying to teach sport specific commands, such as NO, SIT, STAY and COME.
- Like any sport, on hot humid days, it is best to work in the evening and early morning to avoid overheating. Provide plenty of water for both you and your dog. Be aware that arctic and brachycephalic (short nosed) breeds need to be watched closely in the hot weather. Humans also need to be careful to watch for heat related symptoms as well.
- Cold weather may be great for arctic type breeds, but humans should dress appropriately, preferably in layers. It is just as important to hydrate properly in winter months.
- Depending on the type of terrain, dog booties may be needed. This will protect the canines' paws in cold weather preventing ice from accumulating between the pads. It will also protect their paws on rough terrain.

Although many websites will tell you any dog can participate, please be aware of what the dog was bred to do, especially mixed breeds.

Precautions

Precautions:
- See General Precautions
- Remember, with tracking you have to keep up with your dog, so make sure you are prepared to go the distance.
- If you are training a puppy, do not go long distances until you puppy is at least 12 months depending on the breed.
- Depending on the type of terrain, dog booties may be needed. This will protect the canine's feet in cold weather preventing ice from accumulating between the pads. It will also protect their feet on rough terrain.

EARTHDOG	
BREED TYPE and/or BODY TYPE	Short Legged Terriers, such as Parsons (Jack) Russell Terrier, Cairn Terrier, Norfolk or Norwich Terrier, etc.
DESCRIPTION	Earthdog trials were set up for small, short-legged terriers that were primarily bred to hunt vermin and other quarry that lives underground. • Man made tunnels are set up for the dogs to negotiate following the scent of the rat or other quarry. • Rats are caged and unharmed at the end of the tunnel. These dogs must 'work' the tunnel, which may mean barking, scratching, staring, pawing, digging; any active behavior. • According to the AKC General Regulations for Earthdog Tests ,'the noncompetitive program begins with a basic introduction to den work and quarry, progressing through gradual steps to the point where the dog can demonstrate that it is willing to perform the required tasks, including seeking its quarry and working it underground'.
AMERICAN KENNEL CLUB (AKC) TRIALS	Only a certain purebreds may participate in the AKC trials. • They do not have to be intact, but have to be at least 6 months old, females not in heat, and may not be deaf/blind. • Go to the *AKC.org* website for more info. Here is an excerpt from **The AKC Earthdog** section *http://classic.akc.org/events/earthdog/info.cfm* that shows the titles in progressing difficulty. Also see AKC: *https://www.akc.org/sports/earthdog/getting-started/* **Introduction to Quarry** The initial test is the Introduction to Quarry (IQ) where the dog is introduced to a 10 foot tunnel with one right angle turn and at the end is a cage of rats behind a set of bars. • There is a scent trail of rat scent leading into the tunnel and to the rats. At this level the handler can encourage the dog into the tunnel and the judge may help get the dog working at the rats by shaking the cage or making a noise to incite the dog's instincts. **Junior Earthdog** The first level where a title is earned is the Junior Earthdog test where the dog may earn a Junior Earthdog title (J.E.). • The dog must travel a 30 foot den with at least three right angle turns in 30 seconds; work the rats at the end of the tunnel (in a cage behind bars as in IQ)for 60 seconds; and then allow the handler to remove him without injury to the dog or handler. • Once the dog completes these requirements twice under two different judges he will receive the title of J.E. and receive a Junior Earthdog certificate from the AKC. **Senior Earthdog** The second level of Earthdog test is the Senior Earthdog test where the dog may earn a Senior Earthdog title (S.E.). • The den is 30 feet with at least three right angle turns and there are the added distractions of a false, unscented exit and an unscented bedding area with used rat bedding at the end. • The dog has 90 seconds to travel the tunnel length and get to the rats; must begin working the rats within 15 seconds of arriving at the end of the tunnel; and must work the rats for 90 seconds. • At the end of the 90 seconds the rats are removed and the dog must recall from the den to the handler within 90 seconds. • Once the dog completes these requirements under two different judges at three different tests, the dog will be designated a Senior Earthdog (S.E.).

	Master Earthdog The final level of the Earthdog test is the Master Earthdog (M.E.) title. • The dog must actually hunt his way to the den with a bracemate 100 to 300 yards. • On the way he must investigate an empty, unscented den when the handler asks him to. Then both dogs must find the entrance to the den and mark it decisively so that there is no question the dog is indicating an active den. • The den itself is like the Senior den with the addition of two obstacles: a 6 inch diameter PVC pipe crossways in the den to simulate a root and a narrowing down to 6 inches for a distance of 18 inches. • The Master competitor has 90 seconds to get to his quarry; must work the rats for 90 seconds and must allow himself to be removed from the den by his handler within 15 seconds. • While one dog is working the other dog is staked out and must wait his turn with minimum amount of noise while his bracemate works the quarry. • Once a dog successfully completes all parts of the Master test four times under three different judges the dog shall be designated a Master Earthdog and may continue to compete at all three levels at Earthdog tests.
AMERICAN WORKING TERRIER ASSOCIATION (AWTA) TRIALS	The AWTA awards Certificates of Gameness to terriers and Dachshunds who achieve a score of 100% in the AWTA open class. • To qualify in the open class, a dog must be released near the trial's 30-foot (9.1 m) earth tunnel opening, find its way into the tunnel and reach the quarry, all within 30 seconds (50% of score) and then "work" the rat continuously for a full 60 seconds (remaining 50% of score). • Timing starts from the moment the dog is released by the handler. • The dog may enter the tunnel and come out or walk around the tunnel, but it must get to the rat within the time allotted. However, once it reaches the rat, it must remain with it for the aforementioned 60 seconds'. **(See** *https://www.awta.org/* for more information**).**

TRAINING
 	
Canine
	For the most part, your training will be done at the Club you choose. The reason is, the equipment (tunnels) can be very expensive. You must also get yourself a rat and take proper care of it. This means finding a suitable cage that your dog cannot get to, feeding, cleaning, etc. You must also keep the 'prey' in a place your dog cannot see, as he may just lose interest altogether. You can start your training with learning basic commands, esp. the recall command. If you DO want to go through the trouble of setting up a home tunnel, here are some tips to start out.
	
	• Boredom: Whether you are training a puppy or older dog, remember terriers get bored with repetition. Always keep it fun.
	• Tunnel: Start with a straight piece of tubing or PVC pipe that your dog can fit it. As he advances, you may have to construct a tunneling system that allows for turns.
	• Rat: First, check out my website **www.losttemplepets.com - *small animals*)** for info on taking care of rodents. You will need a strong cage to put at the end of the tunnel, preferably inside another wooden cage.
	   o Put the rat on the ground in the cage. Use a leash on the dog to introduce the rat. Use a command like 'Get the Rat' or 'Go' to excite him into getting the rodent.
	   o Move the cage if you must to get him to bark, scratch and aggressively go after the cage.
	   o See if you can get the rats scent on a furry toy and have someone else pull it on a string through the tunnel. Try to get your dog to 'chase' the imitation rat through the tunnel.

- Tunnel training: As above, try to get your dog to go through the tunnel, whether it be chasing the imitation rat or placing yourself at the other end coaxing him to the other side with the rat cage. Tell him to 'Get It' or whatever phrase you have chosen.
  - You may try using a long leash to 'pull' him through but never force him.
  - If you are simply having trouble getting him to go through the tunnel, try putting his favorite toy at the other end, or make a 'treat' trail throughout the tunnel for him to follow to make it a pleasant experience.
  - Once he is comfortable and gets the hint, try making angles for him to go through.
- Underground: If he seems to enjoy this sport, and if you haven't already, it is time for you to join a club and get proper training.

FIELD TRIALS	
BREED TYPE and/or BODY TYPE	Breed Specific (see example of breed in each category)
DESCRIPTION	Field trials cover many hunting events, including retrieval, flushing and pointing. • In field trials, dog and handler teams compete against one another, where there is only one winner in the end. • This requires a higher level of training than a hunting test, where the dog is evaluated against a written standard. • Furthermore, there are many organizations that have their own rules and definitions. • Field trials are also very breed specific. • I will only go over the different types of trials/breeds in this section and some of the equipment you MAY need depending on what type of activity you decide upon. From that point you may want to contact your nearest hunting club for more information and training. **BEAGLE, DACHHUND, FOXHOUND**, or various **HOUND FIELD TRIALS**. These are trials that all have their own rules from single, small packs and large packs to hunt various game. I am not getting into the various trials but just want to make you aware that these exist. If you have a breed that fits these categories, you can contact the appropriate association for more information and training.
PRECAUTIONS	See General Precautions and *Precautions* above in addition to following: • It is important NOT to crate your dog directly after the event, especially if he is coming right out of the water. • Like any sport, your dog should be walked and dried off appropriately before being crated. If you are entering more than one dog, please bring another person to hand the dog off to.
Retrieving	

DESCRIPTION	Retrievers must remember where the bird went down, retrieve the bird from either land or water back to their handler. See breeds below for an example of some of the canines involved in this sport.
	
	Example of Breeds: American water spaniel, Chesapeake Bay retriever, Curly-coated retriever, Flat-coated retriever, Golden retriever, Irish water spaniel, Labrador retriever, Nova Scotia duck tolling retriever, Poodle, Portuguese water dog, Spanish Water dog, etc.
	
	In order to work properly as a gun dog, a retriever should be trained to perform the following tasks:
	   o Remain under Control.
	   o Mark downed game.
	   o Perform a Blind Retrieve.
	   o Retrieve to Hand.
	   o Honoring.
	   o Shake on Command.
	   o Remain Steady to Wing and Shot.

EQUIPMENT	EQUIPMENT • Plastic dummy used specifically for training bird dogs. • Eventually you will need dead birds to training with. • Whistles • Blank pistol (hunter orange) • Appropriate hunter orange equipment, such as vests.

	Flushing

DESCRIPTION	These dogs must first hunt or find the prey and then flush it from its hiding place for the handler to shoot or capture. These dogs can also be used to retrieve the game as well. Spaniels are usually used in this trial, but retrievers are known to do this as well.
	
	Example of Breeds: American cocker spaniel, English cocker spaniel, English Springer spaniel, Field spaniel, Welsh Springer spaniel. Clumber spaniels and Sussex spaniels were bred for certain terrain as well.
	
	The dog needs to be trained to flush the bird, sit when the bird flushes, stay steady with the gun shot, mark where the bird falls and stay until sent to retrieve the game.
	• Spaniels are trained primarily to quarter in front of the hunter to flush game. Trained spaniels should possess the following skills: 
	     ○ Retrieve to Hand.
	     ○ Soft Mouth.
	     ○ Quarter.
	     ○ Scenting
	     ○ Flushing.
	     ○ Hup. *This is the traditional command to sit and stay..*
	     ○ Follow Hand Signals
	     ○ Stead*y.*
	     ○ Blind Retrieve.

EQUIPMENT	EQUIPMENT • Plastic dummy used specifically for training bird dogs. • Bird launcher to simulate a flying bird • Whistles • Blank pistol (hunter orange) • Appropriate hunter orange equipment, such as vests.

	Pointing
DESCRIPTION	Point out the game for the handler to shoot and retrieve the downed bird to the handler. This is done in braces or pairs. Setters and pointers are usually the chosen canine for this sport.  **Example of Breeds:** English setter, German shorthaired pointer, German wirehaired pointer, Gordon setter, Irish setter, pointers, Vizslas, Weimaraner, Wirehaired Pointing Griffon. *"Upon reaching the field, the handler often will cast or direct the dog in a wide circle. Experienced dogs will search the edges of the field knowing that birds are usually found there. This wide run helps to burn off the dog's initial exuberance and may help the dog establish its bearings and form a "background" upon which game smells will be processed.* • *The dog then begins working back and forth, starting near the hunter and slowly ranging out. The dog repeats this process as the hunters move through the field. How far a handler allows the dog to range is a matter of personal preference.* • *When game is detected, a dog freezes, either pointing or crouching. The pointing dog remains motionless until the hunters are in position. Handlers give the command whoa, instructing the dog to remain still. What happens next depends on the dog's training".* **Wikipedia: Gun Dog** *http://en.wikipedia.org/wiki/Gun_dog*
EQUIPMENT	EQUIPMENT • Plastic dummy used specifically for training bird dogs. • Eventually you will need dead birds to training with. • Whistles • Blank pistol (hunter orange) • Appropriate hunter orange equipment, such as vests.

HERDING	
BREED TYPE and/or BODY TYPE	Herding dogs breed specific to type of livestock and job.
DESCRIPTION	Whether you have a dog already that you would like to try herding with, or are looking to buy a herding dog, the first question you have to answer is what are you going to herd? ○ Are you going to be herding sheep or cattle? ○ Are you going to be doing this as a sport entering trials or do you have a farm that you will need a working dog for?
PRECAUTIONS	See General Precautions and *Precautions* above in addition to following: • Keep in mind that dogs can become injured, sometimes fatally from being kicked, etc., usually by herding larger stock, such as cattle. • The working breed and show/companion breeds have differences in their personalities. Although they can make good companions, if you are looking for just a companion or agility dog, do not buy a canine that was specifically bred for herding and vice versa. • Do not have puppies do any extensive training re: jumping or long distance until at least 12-18 months.

TYPES of HERDING	There are several ways dogs herd. Depending on what type of dog you have and the livestock you are herding. There are also dogs that are still a type of sheepdog that will guard the flock, but do not herd.
	
	• **Heelers:** These dogs drive the cattle forward by nipping at their heels. The Australian cattle dog is an example of a heeler.
	  ○ Due to their short stature and ability to stay under a kicking cow, the Welsh corgis and the Swedish Vallhund have also been used to drive cattle.
	• **Headers:** These dogs keep the livestock in a group by going to the head of the animal to stop or turn them.
	  ○ *Strong Eyed:* These dogs tend to stare down the livestock and stay in a crouched position. Some examples are the Border collie and the Australian Kelpies. You do not want a dog that tends to 'stick' his stare - these dogs are OK to hold the livestock, but not good at moving them. These dogs tend to work in larger areas because of their speed and drive.
	  ○ *Loose Eyed:* These dogs stay in an upright position and do not keep constant eye contact. These dogs may use their body language to control the livestock, as well as their bark. These dogs usually work independently, such as the Australian Shepherd.
	• **Versatile:** There are other breeds that are more versatile in herding cattle, goats, geese, sheep, etc. There are also breeds, such as the Australian Kelpie and Koolie that run along the backs of the sheep and are known to head, heel and back.

TRIALS	"*A competitive dog sport in which herding dog breeds move animals around a field, fences, gates, or enclosures as directed by their handlers is called a sheepdog trial, herding test or stockdog trial depending on the area. Such events are particularly associated with hill farming areas, where sheep range widely on largely unfenced land.*" Wikipedia: *https://en.wikipedia.org/wiki/Sheepdog_trial*

COMMANDS	Commands may be indicated by a hand movement, whistle or voice. There are many other commands that are also used when working stock and in general use away from stock.  Herding dog commands are generally taught using livestock as the modus operandi. Urban owners without access to livestock are able to teach basic commands through herding games. These are not the only commands used; there are many variations. In New Zealand each dog has a different set of commands to avoid confusion when more than one dog is being worked at one time.

<ul>
<li>**COME-BYE** *or just bye - go to the left of the stock, or clockwise around them.*</li>
<li>**AWAY TO ME***, or just away or 'way - go to the right of the stock, or counterclockwise around them.*</li>
<li>**STAND** *- stop, although when said gently may also mean just to slow down.*</li>
<li>**WAIT** *- (lie) down or sit - stop.*</li>
<li>**STEADY** *- or take time - slow down.*</li>
<li>**CAST** *- gather the stock into a group. Good working dogs will cast over a large area.*</li>
<li>**FIND** *- search for stock. A good dog will hold the stock until the shepherd arrives. Some will bark when the stock have been located.*</li>
<li>**HOLD** *- keep stock where they are.*</li>
<li>**BARK** *or speak up - bark at stock. Useful when more force is needed, and usually essential for working cattle and sheep.*</li>
<li>**LOOK BACK** *- return for a missed animal.*</li>
<li>**IN THERE** *- go through a gap.*</li>
<li>**WALK UP***, walk on or just walk - move in closer to the stock.*</li>
<li>**THAT'LL DO** *- stop working and return to handler'.*
https://en.wikipedia.org/wiki/Herding_dog</li>
</ul>

TRAINING	Here are some tips, preferably **BEFORE** you buy that herding dog. Just because you have a border collie, this does not necessarily mean he is going to like to herd or be good at it. Do plenty of homework ahead of time.

<ul>
<li>**Find the right trainer:**   Go to herding trials or visit farms that have herding dogs. Asks questions and watch the way they train. Go to several trainers to see their differences and similarities.</li>
<li>**Read:** Learn all you can about herding, as well as the stock you will be herding.</li>
<li>**Socialization:** Make sure your puppy/dog has been well socialized. Bring them around livestock to get them exposed. Always have your puppy/dog on a leash when around livestock.</li>
<li>**Obedience:** Teach the basic commands of sit, stay, come, down, stop. You also may want to teach your dog to bark/stop bark on command. Once you find a good trainer, you can proceed by teaching your puppy other commands as above.</li>
<li>**When to Start**: Every dog matures at a different age. Some dogs will take to it naturally, and you will 'just know'.</li>
<li>**YOU:** You will need just as much training as the dog to know proper body positions, commands, patience and endurance.</li>
<li>**Don't MESS UP:** The biggest mistake YOU can make is to start before YOU know what you are doing. It is hard to break a bad habit once it is imbedded in the dog.</li>
</ul>

TRACKING TRIALS	
BREED TYPE and/or BODY TYPE	Scent hound, although most any dog can have fun with tracking.
DESCRIPTION	Do you have a dog that loves to follow his nose? This may be the sport for you. • Tracking, scent work or any general 'nose' work all require your dog to use his sense of smell. • This skill is used for rescue work, hunting, finding narcotics, Schutzhund training, and detecting some human illnesses. • If you are looking to train your dog for fun, there are also tracking trials.
AKC TRIALS	***AKC* TRACKING REGULATIONS -** "*The purpose of a tracking test is to demonstrate the dog's ability to recognize and follow human scent, a skill useful in the service of mankind.* • *Tracking, by nature, is a vigorous, noncompetitive outdoor sport.* • *Tracking tests demonstrate the willingness and enjoyment of the dog in its work and should always represent the best in sportsmanship and camaraderie by the people involved*". AKC Tracking https://www.akc.org/sports/tracking/

TRAINING	There are many sites on tracking, all having their own ideas. Here are some different ways you can teach your canine companion.
	
	• **In the house:** Basically this is a game of hide and go seek. First you need to associate a toy or food with the word.
	   ○ For instance, take a toy that he enjoys or a Kong filled with treats. Associate the word 'Toy' with the object.
	   ○ Once he has the word association, try putting the toy across the room where he can see it and say "find the toy". When he finds it, praise him.
	   ○ Gradually put it behind some, then in another room, etc. If he does well with this game, he should do OK in the field.
	• **Field training**: Choose a field where there are not any strong scents that will confuse the dog. Early morning is best in a field that has tall, damp grass. There are many articles on what to use to train your dog with. For example, you could use hot dogs, toys, or articles, such as leather gloves or wallet. For this scenario we will use hot dogs, but feel free to use whatever works best. Also have treats handy and plenty of praise.
	   ○ Start by walking a straight line. As the dog gets better at tracking, you can start going off the path.
	   ○ Your dog should not be able to see you lay your track down.
	   ○ Take the hot dog and make sure the scent gets into the grass. Walk a straight line about 75 feet and repeat by making sure the scent of the hot dog stays in the grass. Walk another 75 feet and put the scent of the hot dog on a toy, leather wallet or other object. Repeat this one last time with another object.
	   ○ When you return to the starting place, make sure you follow the same path.
	   ○ It is best to start with a harness/30 foot leash if your dog does not follow commands.
	   ○ Put your dog in the 'down' position and have him get the smell of the article or hot dog. As in house training, tell him to 'find it' or 'look for it'. Point to the ground and encourage him to pick up the scent. When he does praise him and encourage to follow the scent. When he gets to the first scent, repeat to find the first article.

	o When he reaches the first article, try to get him to pick it up and praise him. If needed, give him a treat. Encourage him to the second article and praise when he completes his task. o Not all dogs catch on right away. If he seems to be having problems, try with shorter distances or other articles. As he gets better, try using leather wallets or articles with your scent on it. o If your dog is having trouble keeping his nose down, try using a Bottcher harness to keep him in that position.
EQUIPMENT	• **Harness** A Bottcher harness is made to keep the dogs head down. If this is not a problem with your dog, there are many multi-purpose harnesses you can use. Make sure the harness does not constrict movement. • **Items to Track** This could include a leather wallet or old leather gloves. • **Lead/Line** For training you may need several lengths up to 30-40 feet. You will also need a standard leash.

References

Acme Canine -Training A Dog To Track https://acmecanine.com/training-a-dog-to-track-slow-and-methodical-process/

American Breeder - *How do I train my dog to track scents?*
https://www.americanbreeder.com/resources/american-breeder-blog/dogs/dog-scent-tracking-training-guide

American Kennel Club (AKC): Earthdog https://www.akc.org/sports/earthdog/

American Kennel Club (AKC): Herding https://www.akc.org/sports/herding/

American Kennel Club (AKC): Tracking https://www.akc.org/sports/tracking/

Gundog - How to Train the Dual-Purpose Retriever
https://www.gundogmag.com/editorial/how-to-train-dualpurpose-retriever/466559

Gundog - *How To: Develop A Great Pointing Dog*
https://www.gundogmag.com/editorial/how-to-develop-a-great-pointing-dog/175551

Gundog - *A Balanced Approach to Training Your Flushing Dog*
https://www.gundogmag.com/editorial/balanced-approach-training-flushing-dog/367828

Hepper Blog - *How to Train a Dog to Track: 6 Vet-Approved Steps* - By Brooke Billingsley Updated on October 24, 2025 - https://articles.hepper.com/how-to-train-dog-to-track/

Magic's Legacy – Herding, Instinct Tests - https://www.shannonwolfeherding.com/instinct-tests

Mossy Oak - *Retriever Training and Hunting - How to Train*
By Bill Gibson, Head Trainer of Mossy Oak Gamekeeper Kennels
https://www.mossyoak.com/our-obsession/blogs/dogs/retriever-training-and-hunting-how-to-train

Wikipedia: Gun Dog https://en.wikipedia.org/wiki/Gun_dog

Wikipedia: Herding Dog https://en.wikipedia.org/wiki/Herding_dog

Dirt Dog - AWTA https://www.awta.org/

WATER SPORTS
Quick Summary & Precautions

Dock Diving/Jumping
- If your dog loves the water and has a good toy drive, this may be the sport for you. This is a sport that does require you have access to a dock with a pool, lake, ocean or any large body of water that is deep/long enough, and has enough distance for the dog to get a running start.

Dog Surfing
- Surfing???? Yes surfing. If your dog loves the water, has a lot of energy and takes to the board, why not.

Water Works/Rescue
- Your dog must not only like the water and be comfortable on a boat, but also have the ability to perform the tasks given, as well as be willing to do this on command. He will need to have the instinct to retrieve and also be a strong swimmer.

General Precautions:
- If you are new to the sport, make sure you and your dog get approval by your individual medical professionals as needed (veterinarian or MD)
- Make sure you warm up and cool down as appropriate. A nice walk prior to starting will warm up the muscles. (See the 3rd book in the series on Canine and Human Conditioning)
- If you are training a puppy, make sure they are 12-18 months old before doing any heavy work, depending on the breed.
- If you and/or your canine companion are 'out of shape', please start slow.
- Watch the 'gait pattern' or the way the dog walks before starting. He should have a smooth gait without limping. If you notice any discrepancies in gait before or after starting your sport, check with your vet to make sure there is no arthritis, hip dysplasia or other physical abnormality.
- Your dog should know basic commands before trying to teach sport specific commands, such as NO, SIT, STAY and COME.
- Like any sport, on hot humid days, it is best to work in the evening and early morning to avoid overheating. Provide plenty of water for both you and your dog. Be aware that arctic and brachycephalic (short nosed) breeds need to be watched closely in the hot weather. Humans also need to be careful to watch for heat related symptoms as well.
- Cold weather may be great for arctic type breeds, but humans should dress appropriately, preferably in layers. It is just as important to hydrate properly in winter months.
- Depending on the type of terrain, dog booties may be needed. This will protect the canines' paws in cold weather preventing ice from accumulating between the pads. It will also protect their paws on rough terrain.

Although many websites will tell you any dog can participate, please be aware of what the dog was bred to do, especially mixed breeds.

Precautions

- See General Precautions.
- Be sure your dog is working is a body of water that is safe. There should be no obstacles under the water, as well as being deep enough to prevent injury. If you're diving in a lake, etc, make sure there are no high bacteria levels that can make your dog sick.
- As with other sports, avoid working in hot, humid weather. Also, never have the dog or yourself in a body of water during a storm.
- If you are working in colder weather, make sure your dog is thoroughly dried off after, especially older dogs that are more susceptible to pain from arthritis.

DOCK DIVING / JUMPING

BREED TYPE and/or BODY TYPE	Mesomorphic. Retrievers, water dogs, and some herding/working dogs do well in this sport.
DESCRIPTION	If your dog loves the water and has a good toy drive, this may be the sport for you. • This is a sport that does require you have access to a dock with a pool, lake, ocean or any large body of water that is deep/long enough, and has enough distance for the dog to get a running start. • Any dog may compete, but this is a one size fits all sport. There are no categories for small dogs, as opposed to larger dogs. This is why you see a lot of water retriever type dogs; although I have seen herding dogs and other breeds compete as well. • The dog must be at least 6 months old to compete. • Water retrieval is OK for young dogs, but jumping on land should never be done until the dog is 12-18 months old depending on the breed.
THREE MAIN DISCIPLINES	There are three main disciplines that you can participate in:  **BIG AIR:** Measures distance. • Measurement is taken where the base of the dogs tail hits the water • You are given 90 seconds to complete each jump. • You are given two jumps, the best score (or longest distance) of the two is your final score. **SPEED RETRIEVAL:** Measures speed - timed event • A Flappy (see equipment) is placed at the end of a pool or 38" from the dock. • The dog must stay in a sit/stay position 20' from the edge of the dock. • When the signal is given the dog must jump from the dock and swim to the flappy. • When he reaches the Flappy, he must pull and down and then the time will stop. • Like Big Air, the dog and handler are given 90 sec to execute the run, and the better of two runs will be your final score. **EXTREME VERTICAL:** Measures height • The bumper is hung from an extender 8 feet out from the dock. • The height starts at 4"6' or up as high as the dog can jump. • The bumper is then moved up in increments as each dog jumps. • The dog can start anywhere in front of the 20" line on the dock and has 60 sec to complete jump. • The dog has two chances to complete the jump at each height. • The bumper must be either grabbed by the dog or knocked down completely. If your dog loves all three events, he can enter the IRON MAN competition.

TRAINING	First, make sure your dog likes the water. Find a body of water that is shallow enough to run in and out of. Throw a floatable toy into the water first. 

- Never force your dog into the water or start training when the water is ice cold. Some dogs take a little time, while others just don't like water. You always want to make it fun with positive reinforcements.
- Gradually increase the distance to encourage him to drive into the water for the toy.
- Your dog should know the basic commands of SIT, STAY, and RETRIEVE (or whatever word you choose).
- Put your dog next to you in a sit /stay position, throw the toy into the water to have him retrieve.
- Introducing the Dock: Sit at the end of the dock with your dog. Drop a toy into the water and see if he goes in after it. If not, encourage him, but do not throw the object into the water for distance yet.
    - At first he may just kind of fall or slide off the dock. He may take to this immediately, or it could take weeks for him to get this. Repeat this several times before starting to throw for distance. Make sure you always praise your dog for doing a good job.
- When you think he has this down, start throwing out about 6-8 feet. At this point the dog will still be jumping from the edge of the dock.
- Start backing up when the dog has got the previous step down. Start with 6 feet, 8 feet, etc. Do not keep backing up until he is jumping from the edge of the dock at each distance.
- Once you have the dog jumping it is time to decide what type of technique you will use for your jumps.
    - ***Place and Send***: The handler first throws the object into the pool. The dog starts at the back of the dock and runs/jumps for an object that is already in the pool. The dog does not need a good stay and the handler does not need an accurate throw, but the dog also does not get much height or distance with this technique.
    - ***Chase:*** This is a more popular technique where the dog is in a sit/stay position at the back of the dog. The handler then goes to the front of the dock, releases the dog and throws the object out into the water when the dog is about 4-5 feet from the edge. The dog gets more height and distance, but the handler MUST have a good throw and the dog must stay in a sit position until released.

If you and your dog find that this is the sport for you, check out the clubs in your area to advance your techniques. **Dock Dogs** *www.dockdogs.com*

EQUIPMENT	EQUIPMENT

- **Floatable Toys**
  Any toy that your dog loves that will float on water. If possible, use hunting dummies or bumpers, as they are easy to see.

- **Flappy**
  A type of bumper used in speed retrieval events.

- **Body of Water and Dock**

DOG SURFING

BREED TYPE and/or BODY TYPE	Any dog that loves the sport. Caution with some bull breeds to use a life vest, as they 'sink'.
DESCRIPTION	Surfing???? Yes surfing. If your dog loves the water, has a lot of energy and takes to the board, why not. • There are even competitions with fairly simple rules. • Each canine or canine team is given ten minutes to catch a wave. The contestants are judged based on their confidence, ability to stay on the board and length of ride. • Of course, this sport does require you have access to a beach.
PRECAUTIONS	See General Precautions and *Precautions* above in addition to following: • Make sure your dog has a life vest and has practiced wearing it before getting into the water. • Consider at wet suit for you and your dog if you are in cooler climates.

TRAINING	TRAINING - Here are some basics, but for step-by-step instructions visit **Surf Dog Ricochet at** *surfdogricochet.com*
	
	Just as in dock diving, never force you dog into the water. Some dogs take awhile to get accustomed to salt water, especially if they are used to rivers, lakes or pools.
	• When he is used to the water, introduce him to Small waves first to not overwhelm him. Every time you introduce something, make it fun.
	    o If he backs off from the waves, you need to back off as well.
	• Once you know your dog is comfortable with water it is time to introduce the board.
	• There are different techniques, but personally, I would introduce the board to him at home. Let him stand on the board and explore.
	    o You can also feed your dog on the board and make it a positive experience for him. Put the bowls on the back of the board to reinforce the correct position.
	• *Some dogs can jump on a board in the ocean and surf the first time they try. Others use the surfboard as a diving board and jump off when the board starts to move. Others are a little freaked out by the movement of the board, and it takes them a little longer to get the hang of it. Still others are just used to going to the beach to play ball and aren't quite sure what this new game is all about. See surfdogricochet.com for some great training tips.*
	• At the beginning you can use treats to lure him on the board, but this is only temporary.
	    o Do not force the dog on the board.
	• Dogs can surf in either a sitting, standing or lying position.
	• *'Once your dog is eager to get on the board, you can start introducing a "stay" or "wait" cue. You want your dog to stay on the board even if you aren't near. Because once you push your dog off into a wave, he/she's on their own.*
	    o *You want them to stay on the board, not jump off and swim back to you. When your dog is doing well with the "stay" or "wait"... begin taking steps backwards so you put distance between yourself and the dog. Walk back to the dog to treat on the board.*
	    o *When your dog is comfortable and stays on the board when you step back a couple feet, build upon that until you're able to walk completely around the board.*
	    o *At first you may only get a few steps, but as you progress you'll be able to run around the board while your dog stays on it!' surfdogricochet.com*
	    o Use a release word when you want the dog to get off of the board.

- Introduce distractions that he would find on a beach while practicing.
- Use pillows underneath the board to introduce an unstable surface.
  - This is also a great exercise for core stability that the dog will need in surfing, especially if he surfs standing.
  - You can move the board in several directions and increase the size of the object underneath as he gets used to it but always make this a positive experience.
- Now it is time to hit the water (not literally). Try taking your dog into a small kiddies pool and encourage him to get on the board. This will give him the feel for the water.
- Next introduce the dog to a lake or calm body of water, very shallow. If he gets on, you can pull him out a little deeper. If he seems to enjoy this, it is time for you to join a club to teach your dog how to surf.

If you and your dog find that this is the sport for you, check out the clubs in your area to advance your techniques.

EQUIPMENT	EQUIPMENT
	• **Surfboard** Foam boards work best. 6 foot for smaller dogs and 8 foot for larger. • **Life Jacket** Make sure it fits well, as you will be using it a lot to lift him onto the boat. • **Wet Suit (if needed)** Yes, they do make wet suits for dogs for practicing in cooler climates/water. • **Body of Water with Waves.**

WATER WORKS / RESCUE

BREED TYPE and/or BODY TYPE	Any dog that is a strong swimmer and can pull a human, although this sport is dominated by the Portuguese Water dog and Newfoundland.
DESCRIPTION	Your dog must not only like the water and be comfortable on a boat but also have the ability to perform the tasks given, as well as be willing to do this on command. • He will need to have the instinct to retrieve and also be a strong swimmer. • Water rescue is dominated by working dogs, such as the Newfoundland and Portuguese water dog, but any dog with the physical ability and willingness can participate. • Water works takes a lot of patience, time, and knowledge from the owner as well.
PRECAUTIONS	See General Precautions and *Precautions* above in addition to following: • Dog MUST be a strong swimmer. • Make sure YOU can swim, as you will be in the water at times swimming with your dog. • This is not a book on skill training, so if you are planning on doing SEARCH and RESCUE, make sure you have the appropriate contacts and training before attempting this on your own. • Keep a harness/leash nearby in case the dog gets too tired while swimming or gets caught in some debris, so YOU can rescue HIM. • Make sure your dog has a life vest if necessary and has practiced wearing it before getting into the water. • Consider at wet suit for you and your dog if you are in cooler climates. In some cases this may be too constricting, so again check with organizations first.
SUMMARY OF EXERCISES BY LEVEL	Before starting, here is an excerpt from the **Portuguese Water Dog Club of America - Trial Manual** so you can see what this might include. This manual will also give you plenty of information on the rules of these trials. SUMMARY OF EXERCISES BY LEVEL *Exercise and Time Allowed* **Junior Water Dog** (JWD) Retrieve Dummy from Shore - 1 minute; Board Boat and Ride with Handler - 30 seconds, 30 seconds; Call Dog from Shore to Boat - 2 minutes; Measured Swim with Handler - 2 minutes **Apprentice Water Dog** (AWD) Underwater Retrieve - 1 minute; Retrieve Dummy from Shore - 2 minutes; Dummy Carry, Boat Ride and Recall - 30 seconds, 60' boat ride - 30 seconds; Retrieve Floating Line from Shore - 2 minutes; Measured Time and Distance Swim with Handler - 20 seconds, 2 minutes **Working Water Dog** (WWD) Gear Bag Retrieve - 1 minute; Retrieve Dummy from Boat - 2 minutes; Retrieve Overboard Articles - 3 minutes; Retrieve Dummy between Two Boats - 1 minute; Blind Retrieve Of Floating Line from Boat - 2 minutes **Courier Water Dog** (CWD) Courier Pouch Exchange - 2 minutes; Blind Retrieve Of Floating Line: Boat to Shore - 3 minutes; Directed Double Retrieve From Boat - 3 minutes; Retrieve Fishing Net - 3 minutes; Buoy Ball Placement - 3 minutes **Courier Water Dog Excellent** (CWDX) Dog and handler will qualify two more times at the Courier Water Dog level.

TRAINING	Here are some basics to start you out. • Follow the first few steps of dock diving. This will help you see if your dog likes to retrieve in the water. As mentioned previously, just because you have a Newfoundland, this does not necessarily mean he likes the water. • As the majority of water works consists of retrieval as well, working on this on land is the first step. Have your dog retrieve article of all shapes and sizes. Then you can continue in the water. 　　○ *According to the* **Newfoundland Club of America**, *'the **junior division** exercises are fundamental. The first one, basic control, takes place on dry land. The dog's willingness and ability to perform its owner's bidding are tested with heeling, a recall, and a down stay. The five remaining exercises are performed in the water and consist of retrieving a bumper, retrieving a life jacket or cushion, delivering a rope to a swimming steward, towing a boat, and swimming calmly with a handler. Accomplishing all six tasks results in a Water Dog title, issued by the NCA.* 　　○ *In the **senior division**, the dog must retrieve two articles in the proper order, leap from a boat to fetch a paddle, discriminate between three swimmers and then carry a life ring to the one in distress, retrieve underwater, carry a line from shore to a steward in a boat and then tow that boat to shore, and leap from a boat to save its handler, who has "fallen" overboard. A dog that passes these six exercises adds the title of Water Rescue Dog to its name.'* • As with most sports, make sure your dog knows the basic commands to start, and then focus on the 'fetch', 'release', 'bring back' and stay/release. Recall is very important in water rescue. • Once you know your dog is comfortable with water retrieval, have him start retrieving from a dock (see *Dock Diving* above). Eventually have him retrieve from a boat as well (see *Kayak/Canoe* under Outdoor Activity section).  • Practice in all types of environments like lakes, marshes, ocean and rivers. • When your dog is comfortable in the water, start encouraging him to put his head under and retrieve articles under the water. • For personal rescue, talk to the clubs in your area. Do not attempt to teach your dog without guidance, as you could inadvertently teach him to rescue every swimmer passing by. He must recognize the different between 'swimming' and 'sinking'. If you and your dog find that this is the sport for you, check out the clubs in your area to advance your techniques.
EQUIPMENT	EQUIPMENT Water rescue clubs can give you exact lists of equipment, but here are some examples. • **Boat / Body of water** • **Life Jacket** This may need to be used when first practicing. Make sure it fits well, as you may need to use it to lift him onto the boat. • **Objects to retrieve** Depending on the stage of training, this could include buoys, paddles, life vest, bumper, cushions, rope for towing boat, and eventually a mannequin for rescue.

References

American Kennel Club - *Diving Dogs 101*- https://www.akc.org/expert-advice/sports/diving-dogs-101/

Dixie Dock Dogs https://www.dixiedockdogs.com/#/

Dock Dogs https://dockdogs.com/

Surf Dog Ricochet - *Teach your Dog to Surf*
https://www.surfdogricochet.com/surfing-dogs-teach-your-dog-to-surf.html

Portuguese Water Dog Club of America's Water Trial Manual https://www.pwdca.org /

Newfoundland Club of America https://www.ncanewfs.org/index.html

North America Diving Dogs - https://northamericadivingdogs.com/

World Dog Surfing - https://www.surfdogchampionships.com/

OUTDOOR ACTIVITIES
Quick Summary & Precautions

Dog Hiking/Backpacking
This is great exercise for you and your dog if you enjoy the outdoors. This can be done in all types of weather, short or long distances and with or without a backpack.

Camping
See Backpacking for the Hiking aspect of Camping. As this is not a skills training site, I just have some suggestions if you are camping overnight with your dog.

Kayak/Canoe/Boat
- If you like backpacking and hiking, why not take it one step further - Add a boat to the mix.

General Precautions:
- If you are new to the sport, make sure you and your dog get approval by your individual medical professionals as needed (veterinarian or MD)
- Make sure you warm up and cool down as appropriate. A nice walk prior to starting will warm up the muscles. (See the 3rd book in the series on Canine and Human Conditioning)
- If you are training a puppy, make sure they are 12-18 months old before doing any heavy work, depending on the breed.
- If you and/or your canine companion are 'out of shape', please start slow.
- Watch the 'gait pattern' or the way the dog walks before starting. He should have a smooth gait without limping. If you notice any discrepancies in gait before or after starting your sport, check with your vet to make sure there is no arthritis, hip dysplasia or other physical abnormality.
- Your dog should know basic commands before trying to teach sport specific commands, such as NO, SIT, STAY and COME.
- Like any sport, on hot humid days, it is best to work in the evening and early morning to avoid overheating. Provide plenty of water for both you and your dog. Be aware that arctic and brachycephalic (short nosed) breeds need to be watched closely in the hot weather. Humans also need to be careful to watch for heat related symptoms as well.
- Cold weather may be great for arctic type breeds, but humans should dress appropriately, preferably in layers. It is just as important to hydrate properly in winter months.
- Depending on the type of terrain, dog booties may be needed. This will protect the canines' paws in cold weather preventing ice from accumulating between the pads. It will also protect their paws on rough terrain.

Although many websites will tell you any dog can participate, please be aware of what the dog was bred to do, especially mixed breeds.

Precautions

- See General Precautions.
- Dogs should be at least 12-18 months for most of these activities.
- Never have a dog pull or carry a pack if they have joint problems.

DOG HIKING / BACKPACKING	
BREED TYPE and/or BODY TYPE	Any dog, but careful not to 'overload' smaller breeds.
BACKPACKING ETIQUETTE and TIPS	BACKPACKING ETIQUETTE and TIPS <ul><li>Find out ahead of time trails and parks that allow dogs. Dogs are not allowed in most National Parks.</li><li>Do not put *all* your survival gear in the dog's pack. If you get separated, it doesn't do you any good if your dog has your matches and flashlight.</li><li>Stay on the trail so you and your dog do not disturb the vegetation.</li><li>Always pick up after your dog.<ul><li>Keep in mind you will have to carry the 'poop' with you, so make sure you bring an air tight container to store it in until you have a place to dispose of it.</li><li>If for some reason you did not bring a bag, as a last resort at lease 'bury' the scat somewhere off the trail. The same goes for you.</li><li>Bury away from water supplies as well.</li></ul></li><li>Keep the leash on your dog to prevent him from chasing wildlife.</li><li>Step out of the way when passing horses, other people or other dogs.</li><li>Although they may be a happy dog, try to keep your dog from barking.</li><li>Hazards: See **Hike with your Dog** *http://www.hikewithyourdog.com/page156/page24/page24.html* for info on Rattlesnakes, Bears, Cougars, Ticks, Poison Ivy, and more.<ul><li>This is also a great website for other tips while you are hiking.</li></ul></li><li>MOUNTAIN: If you are hiking in the mountains, keep in mind the change in altitude and temperature-know he warning signs of hypothermia and effects of altitude before going up the mountain.<ul><li>Be prepared to not only bring the appropriate clothing, but also a coat for your dog if necessary. Rest often.</li><li>Avoid letting your dog go in streams, not only is the water freezing, but he will also be coming out into cold temperatures as well.</li></ul></li><li>WINTER: *'Although backpacking in the winter is rewarding, it can be dangerous and generally requires more gear.*<ul><li>*Backpackers may need skis or snowshoes to traverse deep snow, or crampons and an ice axe to cross ice in colder climates. Cotton clothing, which absorbs moisture and chills the body, is particularly dangerous in cold weather, so backpackers stick to synthetic materials or materials that won't hold moisture.*</li><li>*Special low-temperature sleeping bags and tents can be expensive, but will be more comfortable than many layers of warm clothing. However when hiking in cold weather it is always better to hike with varying layers of clothing so that as the body heats up layers can be taken off without causing the wearer to sweat or become very chilled.'* *http://en.wikipedia.org/wiki/Backpacking_(wilderness)*</li></ul></li><li>**Whatever you carry in, you must bring out. Never leave your trash behind.**</li></ul>
DESCRIPTION	This is great exercise for you and your dog if you enjoy the outdoors. <ul><li>This can be done in all types of weather, short or long distances and with or without a backpack.</li><li>Using a backpack on a dog also gives them a purpose, especially for working breeds.</li></ul>

TRAINING	The biggest advice for training on the trails is to make sure you are both in good physical condition before adding packs to either you or your dog.
	• Start out slow on even terrain for a short distance.
	    o Gradually increase the distance and weight of the packs you Both may be wearing.
	    o If you have never hiked before, make sure that both you and your dog are ready for backpacking by starting out in a local area without the pack to test out how you react to the terrain, as well as endurance for both You and your Dog.
	• When introducing the pack to the dog, make sure you let him check it out first.
	    o The dog should not be afraid of the pack and should associate it with something pleasant. You may even want to introduce a harness first to get him used to the feel of something on his back.
	    o When first putting the pack on, do not put anything in it until he gets used to it around the house. Then add crumpled newsprint or packages of dry noodles to let him get used of the sound.
	    o Gradually increase the weight
	• In the beginning start your pack with 20% or less of the dog's body weight. You may want to keep smaller dogs under 30 lbs. or that are not designed for carrying a load at a *lesser* percentage.
	    o You can eventually add weight to the pack, up to 30% of the dog's body weight depending on the breed. Some larger dogs, such as the malamute may eventually be able to carry up to 50%.
	• The first time you go out, trial the pack at 10% body wt. for no more than 2 miles.
	• If you're out in the wilderness, Stay and Come are extremely important. The Leave It and Release command is also very beneficial if your dog wants to chase down a squirrel.
	• Make sure your dog is well behaved. If your dog is not socialized or you do not have good control over your dog, this may not be a place for you. There are many dogs and humans on these trails, and this is not place for a dog fight in the middle of nowhere.

EQUIPMENT	• **Backpack**
	There are different styles made with different materials, but for the most part the backpack will come with a compartment on each side or panniers, of which some can be removed.
	    o Some may come with pockets and some with hydration bladders. Make sure the backpack fits snug, but you should be able to fit two fingers under it when it is filled. The pack should not be sliding or restricting the front or back legs.
	    o When first experimenting with weight, check the dogs skin often, especially pressure points that may irritate the dog. When you fill the pack make sure the contents are evenly distributed on both sides so they are balanced. Use plastic or freezer type bags to store items in inside the saddles in case your dog decides to take a swim. Add reflective tape if needed.
	
	• **Tracking Leash**
	At least 12-15 feet or can use retractable leash. Also collar with ID tags.
	
	• **Bowls/Food/Water** - depending on length of the hike
	DOG: Collapsible bowls for both food and water. Bring 8 oz of water for every 1 hour of hiking. Also bring double the amount of dog due to the fact that it can get knock over.
	PEOPLE: For short hikes, power bars may be an option. For longer hikes, *many hikers use specially manufactured, precooked food that can be eaten hot. It is often sold in large, stiff bags that double as preparation or serving or eating vessels. One common variety of special backpacking food is freeze-dried food, which can be quickly reconstituted by adding hot water. This mixture is then left to rehydrate (and cool somewhat) for a few minutes and agitated occasionally before eating.* http://en.wikipedia.org/wiki/Backpacking_(wilderness)

WATER: Do not rely on drinking out of streams, etc. Unless you have a test kit, the water could contain microscopic bacteria, that can cause illness like Giardia for both you and your dog. There are treatments that people use, such as chemical tablets, boiling, passing through ceramic or pressed solid chemical filters (in conjunction with chemical treatments) or ultraviolent light systems.

- **Dog Waste Bags**
  This is a must. Whatever you take into the woods, you need to take out, and that includes picking up after your dog.

OTHER THINGS TO TAKE:

- Space blanket
- Hat with wide brim
- Flashlight or cyalume light sticks
- Waterproof Matches and lighter
- 2 Quarts minimum water for you. Without water, your whole body starts to suffer.
- Power Bar or other packaged, high-energy food source for you.
- Compass - know how to use it, even if you have a GPS
- Trail guide and maps
- Cell phone
- First aid kit (*for both You and your Dog*)- know how to use it
- Duct tape or athletic tape
- Benadryl - for bee stings and allergic reactions
- Tell somebody where you are going and when you should be back .

CAMPING	
BREED TYPE and/or BODY TYPE	Any dog if you are not using a pack for the dog.
DESCRIPTION	See Backpacking for the Hiking aspect of Camping. • As this is not a skills training site, I just have some suggestions if you are camping overnight with your dog. • If this is your first time camping, I suggest going without your dog. • If you have a tent, set it up in the yard if you have space. You can even sleep overnight to see if you have everything you need. • Remember, if you are hiking or camping, you must carry most of the equipment in your pack.
CAMPING TIPS	Keep your dog leashed at all times. If you wake up at night, you do not want to find that Spot has disappeared. • If you are camping in the winter, and your dog can pull a toboggan, you may want to use this to your advantage for carrying your gear. See *Canine Pulling Sports*. • Brush down your dog before he gets into the tent. • Use glow sticks or LED lights to keep track of your dog at night. • If you are in an area where there may be hunting, put a reflective/orange vest on the dog. • Keep the leash on your dog to prevent him from chasing wildlife

	KAYAK / CANOE / BOAT
BREED TYPE and/or BODY TYPE	Any dog.
DESCRIPTION	See *Backpacking* for the Hiking precautions, etc. See *Water Sports* for water related precautions. If you like backpacking and hiking, why not take it one step further - Add a boat to the mix.
TRAINING	This is not skills training, so make sure you can control a boat, kayak, canoe or whatever watercraft you intend on using before introducing a dog. <ul><li>*Swimming*: Make sure your dog is a strong swimmer before starting out. If your dog enjoys the water and cannot swim, find a high-quality life vest.<ul><li>Train them how to wear and vest before setting out, as well as making sure they are comfortable wearing it. Even a strong swimmer should wear a life vest - you never know if the boat will capsize.</li></ul></li><li>If possible, start training young. Start your puppy around 6 months old playing and swimming in shallow water. It is important that no matter how old the dog, to make sure you make it fun, especially if they are reluctant to go in the water.<ul><li>Don't assume because you have a 'waterdog', like the Portuguese water dog or Newfoundland that they can automatically swim or even enjoy the water. On the other hand, you may find an English bulldog that loves the water (although make sure you have a life vest, as this breed can 'sink').</li></ul></li><li>There are several commands that your dog must be solid in for his safety and yours. He must learn to 'Stay' and 'Release' at your command. This will be important when getting your dog in and out of boat (see below). Leave it is another command that he must know, as there are many things the dog can go after which can be dangerous to you and your dog, as well as the wildlife and people around you. Make sure he knows these commands on land with distractions before starting training on the boat.</li><li>*Getting in and out of the Boat:* Hold the boat still either from a dock or the shore. Find a command that works for you, like IN or UP to encourage the dog to get into the boat.<ul><li>Use the Stay, Sit or Down command - whatever command you use to make sure he stays put. Use the Down or Off command when you are ready to have him get out of the boat - make sure he stays until YOU release him. You can practice this by walking away from the boat for a minute with him in the stay position until you give the command for him to get out.</li></ul></li><li>Once he has learned to get in and out from the shore or dock, it is important that he can get in from the water.<ul><li>If he chooses to jump out of the boat and go for a swim, you don't want him or you to panic when he can't figure out how to get back in. Walk the boat into water that is just deep enough for him to swim and practice from there.</li></ul></li><li>When your dog is following the stay command, it is time for you to launch the boat. Where your dog is sitting really depends on the type of boat.<ul><li>If you have a kayak, he may be able to sit between your legs depending on the size and breed.</li><li>Your dog may be more comfortable at the front of the kayak.</li><li>The middle or opposite end of the canoe would be a good place.</li><li>You can buy a rubber mat to fix to the front of the kayak or the floor of the canoe for traction.</li></ul></li><li>Paddle around near the shore the first few times to see how he reacts. If he seems to enjoy it, go out a little further the next few times.<ul><li>Make sure the water is calm and gradually add distractions before taking the boat out too far.</li></ul></li></ul>

EQUIPMENT	EQUIPMENT
	• **Canoe, Kayak or other watercraft.** This will really be up to you. There are many types of kayaks. Wider kayaks are for the lakes, while the longer kayaks are for the sea. There are kayaks for one or two people and some that you sit on top. If you don't already have one, it is best to go to a dealer who can explain the differences and find one that is just right for your needs. • **Dog Life Jacket** These come in different sizes to fit your dog. You can also get them with insulation if you are not sure what type of environment you will be in. If your dog does a lot of swimming, this is a good precaution because it is hard to see when your dog is getting tired. Dogs can drown. Don't forget YOUR lifejacket as well. • **Leash** It is best to find a floating leash with a buoy-like grip. Do not attach the leash to the boat. It is best to get a belt like is used in skijoring that attaches the dog to you with quick release snaps to release the dog quickly if necessary.  • **Harness/collar with ID tags.** • **Sunscreen** Both you and the Dog. • **Water, food, waste bags** to pick up after the dog, and other items as above in Backpacking - make sure everything is in waterproof bags.

References

AKC – American Kennel Club - *Hiking With Dogs: Tips For Hitting the Trail*
https://www.akc.org/expert-advice/lifestyle/tips-for-hiking-with-your-dog/

AKC – American Kennel Club - *How to Kayak With Your Dog*
https://www.akc.org/expert-advice/health/how-to-kayak-with-your-dog/

Pets that Travel - *Camping with Dogs: Ultimate Guide!*
https://www.petsthattravel.com/camping-with-dogs/

Rover.com - *Dog Kayaks: A Guide to Kayaking with Your Dog (and Which Kayaks Are Best)*
https://www.rover.com/blog/dog-kayaks-a-guide-to-kayaking-with-your-dog-and-which-kayaks-are-best/

Tips for Hiking with your Dog by Hike with your dog http://www.hikewithyourdog.com/page156/page156.html

The Manuel: Take your Dog Hiking by Angele Sionna & Elisabeth Kwak-Hefferan for Backpacker
https://www.backpacker.com/home

PROTECTION SPORTS
Quick Summary & Precautions

Schutzhund
- In German, Schutzhund means 'protection dog', although this sport involves much more than this. Although any size dog can compete, the dog must be large enough to jump a 40 inch hurdle, for example.

French Ring Sport
- French Ring is a protection sport that differs a little from Schutzhund. In F.R. the decoy must wear a bite suit, as the dog is allowed to attack anywhere on the body.

Belgian & Mondio Ring
- Like the Mondio Ring, Belgian Ring has three sections that include obedience, jumping (bursting) and Protection (bite work).

General Precautions:
- If you are new to the sport, make sure you and your dog get approval by your individual medical professionals as needed (veterinarian or MD)
- Make sure you warm up and cool down as appropriate. A nice walk prior to starting will warm up the muscles. (See the 3rd book in the series on Canine and Human Conditioning)
- If you are training a puppy, make sure they are 12-18 months old before doing any heavy work, depending on the breed.
- If you and/or your canine companion are 'out of shape', please start slow.
- Watch the 'gait pattern' or the way the dog walks before starting. He should have a smooth gait without limping. If you notice any discrepancies in gait before or after starting your sport, check with your vet to make sure there is no arthritis, hip dysplasia or other physical abnormality.
- Your dog should know basic commands before trying to teach sport specific commands, such as NO, SIT, STAY and COME.
- Like any sport, on hot humid days, it is best to work in the evening and early morning to avoid overheating. Provide plenty of water for both you and your dog. Be aware that arctic and brachycephalic (short nosed) breeds need to be watched closely in the hot weather. Humans also need to be careful to watch for heat related symptoms as well.
- Cold weather may be great for arctic type breeds, but humans should dress appropriately, preferably in layers. It is just as important to hydrate properly in winter months.
- Depending on the type of terrain, dog booties may be needed. This will protect the canines' paws in cold weather preventing ice from accumulating between the pads. It will also protect their paws on rough terrain.

Although many websites will tell you any dog can participate, please be aware of what the dog was bred to do, especially mixed breeds.

Precautions

- See General Precautions
- Due to the nature of the sport, keep an eye on the jaw, mouth and neck for injuries.
- If you are training your dog, you must also be in shape physically, as well as mentally.

SCHUTZHUND

BREED TYPE and/or BODY TYPE	Working dogs, to include breeds like the German Shepherd, Malinois, Giant Schnauzer, Rottweiler, Black Russian Terrier, Tervuren, Beauceron, Doberman Pincher.
DESCRIPTION	In German, Schutzhund means 'protection dog', although this sport involves much more than this.  • Although any size dog can compete, the dog must be large enough to jump a 40 inch hurdle, for example. Unlike agility trials the equipment is not adjusted per size of the dog. This is why you will see larger breeds, such as the German shepherd and Giant Schnauzer. • The dog must also pass "a temperament test called a B or BH (Begleithundprüfung, which translates as "traffic-sure companion dog test"). The B tests basic obedience and sureness around strange people, strange dogs, traffic, and loud noises. A dog that exhibits excessive fear, distractibility, or aggression cannot pass the B and so cannot go on to Schutzhund'. *http://en.wikipedia.org/wiki/Schutzhund* . There are three titles: Sch H I (novice); Sch H II (intermittent) ; Sch H III (Master). A *properly trained* Schutzhund dog will also make a great family pet as well. • Although any dog can participate, make sure your dog has the following traits: Trainable, intelligent, strong bond to handler, protective instinct (not aggressive), courageous, and a strong desire to work. • This is not a sport for an aggressive dog or one that does not obey commands. • Unless you are hiring a handler, you must also be willing to be patient, consistent with commands and dedicated to the sport.
TRAINING PHASES	**TRAINING PHASES**: This is a sport where you really need to join a club for proper training, but these are the phases. Here is a website that may help: *http://www.schutzhund-training.com/lines.html* **Tracking:** *The tracking phase tests not only the dogs scenting ability, but also its mental soundness and physical endurance.* **Obedience***:* *The obedience phase is done in a large field, with the dogs working in pairs. One dog is placed in a down position on the side of the field and his handler leaves him while the other dog works in the field. Then the dogs switch places. In the field, there are several heeling exercises, including heeling through a group of people.* • *There are two or three gunshots during the heeling to test the dog's reaction to loud noises.* • *There are one or two recalls, three retrieves (flat, jump and A-frame), and a send out where the dog is directed to run away from the handler straight and fast and then lie down on command.* • *Obedience is judged on the dog's accuracy and attitude. The dog must show enthusiasm. A dog that is uninterested or cowering scores poorly.* **Protection:** *In the protection phase, the judge has an assistant, called the "decoy", who helps him test the dog's courage to protect himself and his handler and his ability to be controlled while doing so. The decoy wears a heavily padded sleeve on one arm.* *http://en.wikipedia.org/wiki/Schutzhund*

COMMANDS in ENGLISH to GERMAN	COMMANDS **Heel** - Fuss (fooss) **Sit** - Sitz (siitz) **Stay** - Bleib (bly'b) **Down** - Platz **Come/Here** - Hier (hee er) **Stand** - Steh (shtay) **Retrieve/Fetch** Bring (brrring) **Jump** - Hopp **Go Out** - Voraus (for owss) **Track** - Such (tsuuk) **Guard Pass** - auf/Wache **Bite** - Packen/Fass **Out/Let Go** - Aus (owss) **Speak/Bark** - Gib Laut (geblout) **Narcotics/Dope** - Rauschgift **Find narcotics** - Such Rauschgift **Building/Blind** - Search Voran/Revier **Kennel/Crate** - Zwinger/Box **Go Outside** - Geh Raus/Geh Draussen **Go Ahead** - Geh Voraus **Go Inside** - Geh rein (gay rine) **What is going on?** - Was ist los? **Good** (praise) - So ist brav **Correction Word** "No" - Pfui (fooey) Nein (nine) **Don't do that!** - Lass das sein **OK-** In Ordnung **Eat food** - Nimm Futter **Helper Stand Still** - Bleiben Ruhig/Steht Noch **Article Search** - Such Verloren **Leave it** - Lass es	

EQUIPMENT	EQUIPMENT • **Harness** *PROTECTION*: You will need a sturdy harness for you to hold onto. Make sure the harness disperses the pressure across the chest instead of the neck. Padding will help for extra comfort. I also suggest a strong D ring for the leash. **TRACKING:** A Bottcher harness is made to keep the dogs head down. If this is not a problem with your dog, there are many multipurpose harnesses you can use. • **Fur Saver Collar** Although this is a type of 'choke collar', it is usually not used for that purpose, as the leash is usually attached to the D ring. o In competition, regular collars are not allowed. These can be made from several metals, but if your dog is light colored or has any skin allergies, stainless steel is your best bet. • **Lead/Line** Standard leash and a 33-foot tracking line. • **Tug Toys / Dumbbells (different weights)** These are good training tools. For example, your dog will need to carry different weighted dumbbells over a ramp and retrieve on flat ground. • **Bite Sleeves, Ramp, etc.** These are some of the items you may need when you get past the initial training of the sport.

FRENCH RING SPORT	
BREED TYPE and/or BODY TYPE	Working dogs, to include breeds like the German Shepherd, Malinois, Giant Schnauzer, Rottweiler, Black Russian Terrier, Tervuren, Beauceron, Doberman Pincher. Like the above sport, any dog can participate (see Schutzhund above), but Malinois and Dutch Shepherds tend to do well in this sport over German Shepherds because there is a lot more agility and speed in F.R.
DESCRIPTION	French Ring is a protection sport that differs a little from Schutzhund. <ul><li>In F.R. the decoy must wear a bite suit, as the dog is allowed to attack anywhere on the body.</li><li>The exercises are random and not broken up as in Schutzhund, and there is no tracking portion.</li><li>To participate in French Ring Sport, a dog must first pass the Certificat de Sociabilité et d'Aptitude à l'Utilisation (Certificate of Sociability and Aptitude for Work) temperament test.</li><li>There are three levels which include Brevet, Ring I, Ring II and Ring III. Each introduces progressively more difficult situations and makes greater demands from the dog.</li><li>The trial is divided into three sections: Jumps, Breaking in exercises, and protection'. The jumps come first, followed by obedience and then protection.</li></ul> For more information look up the **North American Ring Association NARA** *http://www.ringsport.org/index.php?pg=ringsport*
TRAINING PHASES	This is a sport where you really need to join a club for proper training, but here are some of the events the dog should be able to do when reaching Ring III . <ul><li>Heel on a leash</li><li>Heel with muzzle</li><li>Long sit/down</li><li>Food refusal</li><li>High Jump</li><li>Palisade</li><li>Long Jump</li><li>Thrown Retrieves</li><li>Unseen Retrieve</li><li>Seen Retrieve</li><li>Send Away</li><li>Face Attack</li><li>Fleeing Attack</li><li>Defense of Handler</li><li>Attack with Gun</li><li>Search, Hold, and Bark with Escort</li><li>Stopped Attack</li><li>Guard of Object</li></ul>
EQUIPMENT	EQUIPMENT for Ring Sports - See Schutzhund (Do not need tracking gear) <ul><li>Bite Suit</li></ul>Here are a few websites for more information: Dantero Malinois: *https://dantero.com/* All American K9: *https://all-americank-9.com/* North American Ring Association NARA: *http://www.ringsport.org/index.php?pg=ringsport*

MONDIO and BELGIAN RING SPORT

BREED TYPE and/or BODY TYPE	Working dogs, to include breeds like the German Shepherd, Malinois, Giant Schnauzer, Rottweiler, Black Russian Terrier, Tervuren, Beauceron, Doberman Pincher. Like the above sport, any dog can participate (see Schutzhund above), but Malinois and Dutch Shepherds tend to do well in this sport over German Shepherds because there is a lot more agility and speed in F.R.
MONDIO **DESCRIPTION** **TRAINING**	This is a protection ring sport that tests coordination and precision. • Although like all ring sports, any breed can join, it is dominated again by the Malinois. • As with French Ring Sport, this sport has more hurdles and jumps than Schutzhund. • There are three sections: Obedience, Jumps, and Protection. TRAINING: This is a sport where you really need to join a club for proper training,
BELGIAN **DESCRIPTION** **TRAINING**	Like the Mondio Ring, Belgian Ring has three sections that include obedience, jumping (bursting) and Protection (bite work). • Also like the other sports, any dog that is able to participate physically and mentally are able to compete, although this sport is also dominated by the Malinois. TRAINING: This is a sport where you really need to join a club for proper training, See **Leeburg- The Exercises and Scores in the Belgium Ring** By Germain Pauwels *https://leerburg.com/bel-ring1.htm* for more information

References

All American K9: https://all-americank-9.com/

Canadian Ring Sport - The Basic Philosophy of Ring Sport by Jean-Michel Moreau & Chris Redenbach, 1991 https://www.canadianringsport.ca/philosophy-of-french-ring/

Dantero Malinois: https://dantero.com/articles/

K-9 Evolution - Mondio Ring
https://k9evolutionsdogtraining.com/blog/all-about-mondio-

Leeburg- The Exercises and Scores in the Belgium Ring By Germain Pauwels https://leerburg.com/bel-ring1.htm

North American Ring Association NARA: http://www.ringsport.org/index.php?pg=ringsport

Schutzhund Training. com https://schutzhund.uk/fullscreen/fullscreen-slideshow-2/

United Schutzhund Club of America https://www.germanshepherddog.com/about/schutzhund-

training / **Wikipedia – Schutzhund** - https://en.wikipedia.org/wiki/Schutzhund

POPULAR SPORTS
Quick Summary & Precautions

Lure Coursing
- In lure coursing, a dog chases an artificial lure across a field that is approximately 600-1000 yards long.

Agility
- It is an athletic event that requires conditioning, concentration, training and teamwork. Dog and handlers negotiate an obstacle course racing against the clock.

Flyball
- It is basically a relay race in which dogs run over hurdles about 10 feet apart for a total of 51 feet to get a tennis ball that is released from a box and return it to the start.

Disc Dog
- In disc dog (or *Frisbee*, registered name of a Mattel product), a human thrower controls the disc for the dog to catch. The two most popular events are Catch and Retrieve (or Toss and Fetch) and Freestyle.

Treibball
- The purpose of the game is to drive 8 45-75 cm exercise balls into a soccer sized goal using herding and obedience commands.

General Precautions:
- If you are new to the sport, make sure you and your dog get approval by your individual medical professionals as needed (veterinarian or MD)
- Make sure you warm up and cool down as appropriate. A nice walk prior to starting will warm up the muscles. (See the 3rd book in the series on Canine and Human Conditioning)
- If you are training a puppy, make sure they are 12-18 months old before doing any heavy work, depending on the breed.
- If you and/or your canine companion are 'out of shape', please start slow.
- Watch the 'gait pattern' or the way the dog walks before starting. He should have a smooth gait without limping. If you notice any discrepancies in gait before or after starting your sport, check with your vet to make sure there is no arthritis, hip dysplasia or other physical abnormality.
- Your dog should know basic commands before trying to teach sport specific commands, such as NO, SIT, STAY and COME.
- Like any sport, on hot humid days, it is best to work in the evening and early morning to avoid overheating. Provide plenty of water for both you and your dog. Be aware that arctic and brachycephalic (short nosed) breeds need to be watched closely in the hot weather. Humans also need to be careful to watch for heat related symptoms as well.
- Cold weather may be great for arctic type breeds, but humans should dress appropriately, preferably in layers. It is just as important to hydrate properly in winter months.
- Depending on the type of terrain, dog booties may be needed. This will protect the canines' paws in cold weather preventing ice from accumulating between the pads. It will also protect their paws on rough terrain.

Although many websites will tell you any dog can participate, please be aware of what the dog was bred to do, especially mixed breeds.

Precautions

- See General Precautions
- Never have a dog run or jump if they have joint problems.

LURE COURSING	
BREED TYPE and/or BODY TYPE	Sight hounds – see list below for dogs that are allowed to participate.
DESCRIPTION	Do you have a sight hound that loves to run? This may be for you. • In lure coursing, a dog chases an artificial lure across a field that is approximately 600-1000 yards long. • It may have jumps depending on the association sponsoring the event, but all have turns to simulate chasing a hare, etc.
PRECAUTIONS	See General Precautions and *Precautions* above in addition to following: • If you are training a puppy, make sure they are 12 months old and their growth plates have closed before doing any serious turns. • If your canine companion is 'out of shape', please start slow. Slowly build up his endurance by having him run in a 'safe' field. • Running on asphalt can be harsh on both you and your dog. Try dog booties during practice if needed. • Start your training with ONE dog until he gets understands, then can add another if you want.

ORGANIZATIONS
 	
AMERICAN KENNEL CLUB
	AMERICAN KENNEL CLUB
	
	Lure coursing is an event for all Sighthounds : Afghan Hounds, Basenjis, Borzois, Greyhounds, Ibizan Hounds, Irish Wolfhounds, Italian Greyhounds, Pharaoh Hounds, Rhodesian Ridgebacks, Salukis, Scottish Deerhounds, and Whippets are eligible.
	• *The AKC offers this program that the dogs and owners love so well, to test the dogs basic coursing instinct or hunting by sight ability. The dogs chase an artificial lure, in an open field and are judged by two judges, on the dogs overall ability, speed, endurance, agility, and how well they follow the lure.*
	• *The dogs can earn titles, such as Junior Courser (JC), Senior Courser (SC), and Master Courser (MC). They can also obtain a Field Championship (FC) and the title of Lure Courser Excellent (LCX).*
	• *The upside of this event is the dogs are kept in such good healthy shape, by doing something that comes naturally and that they really like to do. Dogs must be one year old and any dog with a breed disqualification may not participate. https://www.akc.org/sports/coursing/lurecoursing/*
	
	Must be one year or older, females not in heat, and of an eligible breed (see breeds below). Can be spayed or neutered.
	• Tests:
	    ○ Junior Courser (JC): Dogs run by themselves 600 yards with four turns. Must be done under two different judges.
	    ○ Senior Courser (SC): Must have JC title, run with at least one other dog, run four AKC tests under two different judges.
	    ○ Master Courser: 25 qualifying scores in the Open, Open Veteran or Specials Stake and have a Senior Courser Title.
	• In AKC trials hounds are judged for overall ability (10), follow (10), speed (10), agility (10), and endurance (10) for a maximum score of 50 points.

AKC Recognized Breeds
- Afghan Hound
- Azawakh
- Basenji
- Borzoi
- Cirneco Dell'Etna
- Greyhound
- Ibizan Hound
- Irish Wolfhound
- Italian Greyhound
- Pharaoh Hound
- Portuguese Podengo Pequeno
- Rhodesian Ridgeback
- Saluki
- Scottish Deerhound
- Sloughi
- Whippet

Miscellaneous Group*
- Norrbottenspets
- Portuguese Podengos (Medio & Grande)
- Peruvian Inca Orchid

Foundation Stock Service Breeds*
- Thai Ridgeback

*** May compete for suffix titles only**
- Dogs of these breeds recorded with the Purebred Alternative Listing Program/Indefinite Listing Privilege (PAL/ILP) or dogs with Conditional registration are eligible to participate.
- Spayed and neutered dogs are eligible to participate.
- Monorchid and cryptorchid dogs are ineligible to participate.
- Bitches in season are not eligible to participate.
- Hounds with breed disqualifications, as listed in the AKC Breed Standards, are ineligible to enter lure coursing trials and tests.
- Dogs with Limited Registration are eligible to participate.

Eligible AKC breeds. See *http://www.akc.org/events/lure_coursing/eligible_breeds.cfm* for stock breeds and other rules.

ORGANIZATIONS	**AMERICAN SIGHTHOUND FIELD ASSOCIATION (ASFA)**

AMERICAN SIGHTHOUND FIELD ASSOCIATION	*https://asfa.org/coursing.htm*
	
	 - 'A dog must be *Certified* in order to compete in the Open category of the breed. To certify, a dog must run *clean* (not interfere with the other hound and pursue the lure) with another dog of similar running style and be certified by a qualified ASFA judge. Dogs used for certification do not have to be certified themselves, nor do they have to be a sight hound, and judges can certify two or three hounds at the same time'. Wikipedia:_ *http://en.wikipedia.org/wiki/Lure_coursing*
	 - Trials:
	  o Field Championship (FCh): Open hound receives 100 title points plus either two first placements or one first and two second placements.
	  o Lure Courser of Merit (LCM): Hound earns 300 points and four first placements. Each subsequent LCM is earned in the same way.
	 - Follow (15), Enthusiasm (15), Agility (25), Speed (25), Endurance (20)
	 - Normally run in trios with pink, yellow and blue blankets to identify. Eligible AKC breeds.
	 - Eligible Breeds - See AKC above. ASFA also accepts participation from the follow breeds:
	  o Azawakh (Tuareg Sloughi), Deerhounds, Sloughis, Chart Polski, Cirneco dell'Etna, Galgo Espanol, Magyar Agar, Peruvian Inca Orchid, Portuguese Podengo (3 varieties that are to be run separately), Silken Windhound

TRAINING	This is one sport where you either have it or you don't. Most sight hounds take naturally to this sport.
	• As with all sports, make sure your hound knows his basic commands, and has good recall. This is important to call your dog after the race.
	• Test his instincts by tying a piece of cloth, rabbit fur or plastic bag to the end of a string and see if your dog chases it. If she does, you are good to go. If not, try a squeaky toy or treat and have her chase it. Let her catch it at the end to keep her interest.
	• Bring your puppy at about 5 months old to the test field and see if they will let you run a practice course after the race. Only do this on a straight run in the beginning. After your dog is old enough, you can start practicing turns.
	• Practice on different terrains so your dog can adjust accordingly to the test fields.
	• According to the **Hawaii Lure Coursing Club** here are several categories that your dog may fall into:
	   o **Coursers**: *Born to chase a lure.*
	   o **Short Attention Span:** *These dogs will chase for awhile and then lost interest or come back to mom or dad.*
	   o **Hunters:** *Hunting dogs that are very scent driven will get excited, but when they realize that the lure is a bag, will give up.*
	   o **String biters:** *These dogs will get frustrated when they can't catch the lure and will start biting at the string.*
	   o **Pulley biters:** *They get excited at the whirring of the pulleys and abandon the course to attack the pulleys.*
	• There are other dogs that become 'lure wise' where they may try to cheat by cutting off the lure instead of following.

EQUIPMENT	• **Lead** Slip lead to release the dog at the start line. connection between you and your dog. • **Lure** Plastic bag, fur or piece of cloth on a string for practice. • **Blankets** In ASFA Yellow, Pink and Blue blankets are used to identify each dog.

	AGILITY
BREED TYPE and/or BODY TYPE	Mesomorphic, Ectomorphic or Pituitary Dwarf.
DESCRIPTION	*Agility according the AKC:* • *Agility is a sport that appeals to all dog lovers - from young people to senior citizens. It has great spectator appeal. Agility is designed to demonstrate a dog's willingness to work with its handler in a variety of situations. It is an athletic event that requires conditioning, concentration, training and teamwork. Dog and handlers negotiate an obstacle course racing against the clock.* • *The AKC offers three types of agility classes. The first, Standard Class, includes contact objects such as the dog walk, the A-frame, and seesaw. Each of the contact obstacles has a "safety zone" painted on the object and the dog must place at least one paw in that area to complete the obstacle. The second is Jumpers with Weaves. It has only jumps, tunnels and weaves poles with no contact objects to slow the pace. The third is FAST, which stands for Fifteen and Send Time. This class is designed to test handler and dog teams' strategy skill, accuracy, speed and distance handling.* • *All classes offer increasing levels of difficulty to earn Novice, Open, Excellent and Master titles. After completing both an Excellent Standard title and an Excellent Jumpers title, handler and dog teams can compete for the MACH - faster than the speed of sound! (Master Agility Championship title.)* • *A trial is a competition. Clubs hold practice matches and then apply to be licensed to hold official trials. At a licensed trial, handlers and dogs can earn scores toward agility titles.* • *AKC agility is available to every registerable breed. From tiny Yorkshire Terriers to giant Irish Wolfhounds, the dogs run the same course with adjustments in the expected time and jump height.* • *The classes are divided by jump heights in order to make the competition equal between the different sizes of dogs.* **AKC:** *https://www.akc.org/sports/agility/*

PRECAUTIONS	See General Precautions and *Precautions* above in addition to following:
	
	• Make sure you warm up and cool down as appropriate. A nice walk prior to starting will warm up the muscles. Make sure you take a short walk after you compete as well to cool down.
	• If you are training a puppy, make sure they are 12-18 months old before doing any heavy work, especially jumping, depending on the breed.
	• Never have a dog jump if they have joint problems.
	• Your dog should know basic commands before trying to teach sport specific commands, such as NO, SIT, STAY and COME.
	• If you were to evaluate your dog's current level of fitness, what would you look for? There is a great book by **Christine Zink** called **Peak Performances.** Here are some of the things she suggests to evaluate your dog's current level of fitness before starting an agility program.
	    o What body type is the dog (endomorphic, etc).
	    o Does he have appropriate front and rear angulations for the breed? You may want to check with a breeder if it is a purebred for the standard.
	    o Look for any structural faults that should be paid attention to before starting a program.
	    o Does he have good muscle tone or he is overweight. Check the dog's tone and see if it is it the same bilaterally or is he favoring one side over the other.

	o Have the dog checked by a vet for any congenital or new conditions that may affect his performance or be exacerbated by an exercise program. o Learn to identify early signs of fatigue and know when not to push the dog. ***(Zink, 2004, pp. 111-112)*** • As this book suggests, it is just as important that you are able to keep up with your dog. In agility, you will have to run forward/backwards and make sudden changes in direction. Human agility and strength training will help prevent injury in yourself as well. • Weight: It is the taboo word, but keeping the weight down will put less stress on joints with jumping.
TRAINING	As this is not a book on skills training, please go to one of the many agility clubs in your area. Here are a couple of things to keep in mind when training • As previously mentions, if you are training a puppy, you can start to teach balance on a stability ball or rocker board at a young age. Try putting some PCV pipes on the ground and guide him over to teach front and hind end awareness. Do NOT have them start jumping or running up steep obstacles until they are mature. • Ask if you can bring your dog to the agility facility with no one there first to introduce him to the equipment. If he is hesitant to get near the equipment, bring him a few more times – use a leash if necessary to bring him to each piece and have him walk over the frames and use the teeter without any distractions. • Once he is comfortable with the area, bring him to a few classes to see how he responds with other dogs around. • Some dogs will be timid, while others see this as simply a place to play. Agility should *always* be fun for both you and your dog, but you also want to make sure your dog knows the 'etiquette' rules when entering the agility facility. o Be respectful of other dogs – some dogs do not like you to 'invade their space'. o Do not assume all other trainers use treats – keep a dog pouch on your belt and pick up after any treats that may fall during training. o Keep your dog on a leash until it is your turn to 'run'. • If your dog 'fears' an obstacle, do not make a big deal out of it (positive or negative). You obviously do not want to yell at the dog for fearing it, but at the same time do not baby him and show positive reinforcement to his fear. For example, a small dog (or large) may not want to go through the chute. Try creative techniques like pulling a treat through the other end on a string while lifting the chute slightly so he can see that there is a 'light' at the end of the tunnel. • As with all sports, it is easier to get all the facts ahead of time and teach your dog correctly the first time, as it is difficult to undo bad habits.
EQUIPMENT	EQUIPMENT or Obstacles: (Description by *Wikipedia http://en.wikipedia.org/wiki/Dog_agility*  • **A-Frame** Two broad ramps, usually about 3 feet (0.91 m) wide by 8 to 9 feet (2.7 m) long, hinged together and raised so that the hinged connection is between five and six-and-a-quarter feet above the ground (depending on the organization), roughly forming an A shape. • **Dogwalk** Three 8 to 12 ft (2.4 to 3.7 m) planks, 9 to 12 inches (23 to 30 cm) wide, connected at the ends. The center plank is raised to about 4 feet (1.2 m) above the ground, so that the two end planks form ramps leading up to and down from the center plank. This obstacle also has contact zones. Most sanctioning organizations also require slats on the dog walk ramps. • **Teeter** A 10-to-12-foot (3.0 to 3.7 m) plank pivoting on a fulcrum, much like a child's seesaw.

- **Jump (or hurdle)**
  Two uprights supporting a horizontal bar over which the dog jumps.
- **Double and triple jump** (or spread jump)
  Two uprights supporting two or three horizontal bars spread forward or back from each other.
- **Panel jump**
  Instead of horizontal bars, the jump is a solid panel from the ground up to the jump height, constructed of several short panels that can be removed to adjust the height for different dog heights.
- **Broad jump** (or long jump)
  A set of four or five slightly raised platforms that form a broad area over which the dog must jump without setting their feet on any of the platforms
- **Tire jump**
  A torus shape roughly the size of a tire, suspended in a frame.
- **Open Tunnel**
  A vinyl tube, 10 to 20 feet (3.0 to 6.1 m) long and about 2 feet (61 cm) in diameter, through which the dog runs.
- **Closed Tunnel or chute**
  A barrel-like cylinder with a tube of fabric attached around one end. The fabric extends about 8 to 12 feet (2.4 to 3.7 m) and lies closed until the dog runs into the open end of the chute and pushes his way out through the fabric tube.
- **Weave Poles**
  Similar to a slalom, this is a series of 5 to 12 upright poles, each about 3 feet (0.91 m) tall and spaced about 20 inches (51 cm) apart, through which the dog weaves.
- **Table**
  An elevated square platform about 3-foot-by-3-foot (1-meter-by-1-meter) square onto which the dog must jump and pause, either sitting or in a down position, for a designated period of time which is counted out by the judge, usually about 5 seconds.

FLYBALL	
BREED TYPE and/or BODY TYPE	Mesomorphic or Pituitary Dwarf
DESCRIPTION	Flyball is a sport that incorporates a team of dogs instead of working individually. • This is a sport that requires focus on your dog's part and is truly a team sport. It is basically a relay race in which dogs run over hurdles about 10 feet apart for a total of 51 feet to get a tennis ball that is released from a box and return it to the start. At this point another dog takes over for a total of 4 dogs on each team. • Any dog can participate, although you will see many border collies and terriers. • As the jumps are measured 4 inches below the withers of the smallest dog, it is usually wise to have a small dog as a part of the team. • In order to get the tennis ball, the dog must press a spring-loaded pad that may be difficult for some small dogs, which may need to jump their whole body onto the board. • Each dog must also cross the start line before the other dog can start. Usually, two similarly timed teams will compete at a time. There are two main organizations that include the original North American Flyball Association (NAFA) and a newer one called United Flyball League International (U-FLI). Competitions are usually hosted by local flyball clubs.
PRECAUTIONS	See General Precautions and *Precautions* above in addition to following: Pushing on the box can put a lot of stress on the dog's wrist, especially in smaller dogs that need to put more pressure. • Dogs usually turn in one direction, so it is important that you practice with your dog doing figure eights for example in the opposite direction. For example, if your dog always turns left, he can have cervical problems and tightened muscles on that side. • TMJ (Jaw) problems from grasping the ball with his mouth. • Other problems that can arise from this sport are problems with the lower back, back hock and iliopsoas.
TRAINING	Here are some suggestions as to how to start training your dog. As always, this is not a book on skills training, so contact your local club for more information. • Have one person holding onto the dog, facing the opposite direction. The owner or handler should run in the other direction towards the box while he is released and allowed to chase him. • Now put one hurdle in between and repeat as above. If the dog is reluctant, try having the first person put him on a leash and run beside him to coax him over the hurdle the first few times. Praise the dog every time he reaches the handler. • Gradually add more hurdles until the correct number of hurdles is consistently jumped. This may take several hours, days or weeks for the dog to get to this point. • Once he has this down and is consistently getting to the box, try reversing this action. • If needed, put a guard or some type of fencing on either side to keep the dog from going off track. • Now try putting the ball on the ground for the dog to grab and bring back. You may need a person on one side and you on the other to keep this 'game' going back and forth. • When you add the Flyball box into the mix, let your dog see that you are putting the ball in the box. When he pushing on the box, it will naturally release. Again, this is not going to happen in one day, so don't give up. There may be many other training methods out there for teaching you and your dog, so read up, go on websites and talk to your local Flyball club.
EQUIPMENT	EQUIPMENT • Jumps Jumps should be measured 5 inches below the smallest dog's withers (on your team). • Flyball Box • Tennis Balls (use a ball made for dogs) It is better to practice with the size ball you will be using in competition.

DISC DOG	
BREED TYPE and/or BODY TYPE	Mesomorphic
DESCRIPTION and EVENTS	In disc dog (or *Frisbee*, registered name of a Mattel product), a human thrower controls the disc for the dog to catch. • The two most popular events are Catch and Retrieve (or Toss and Fetch) and Freestyle. **EVENTS:** • ***Toss and Fetch***: Contestants have 60 seconds to make as many throws as possible on a field marked with increasingly longer distances. One disc is thrown and dogs get points for catching the disc depending on distance and catching in mid air. • ***Freestyle:*** Teams are judged subjectively based on degree of difficulty, showmanship, and athleticism. Events can include skateboard, freestyle hackysack and snowboard halfpipe.
PRECAUTIONS	See General Precautions and *Precautions* above. In addition to following: See Precautions above, and with agility. • 60-70% of the dog's weight on the front legs. Because dog's are built to put the weight on the front legs when landing, it is important to throw 'low' as much as possible to avoid putting stress on the back legs. Teach your dog to land 'flat' and not to have him twist. • This is one of those sports where YOU need to pay close attention to YOUR body mechanics. It is important that you have a strong 'core' before trying advanced moves, like having a dog jump on your back. • This book is not on skills training, so make sure You know how to throw a disc or 'Frisbee' before having your dog try to catch it. • The best disc dogs will be of a lean build about 30-50 lbs. with strong retrieval and tracking skills. • Do NOT throw the disc directly at the dog. • As above, make sure you dog is at least 14–15-month-old, depending on the breed, before having him do any jumping. • Put the discs away so the dog knows that they are only used for this particular game.
TRAINING	As this is not a book on skills training, please go to one of the many disc dog clubs in your area. Here are a couple of things to keep in mind when training. • First, get the dog acquainted with the disc. He needs to see it as nonthreatening. You can even use it as a feeding dish in the beginning. • Crouching at his level, move the disc around to get his attention. You can then try rolling it on the ground to see if he will go after it. Praise him if he goes after the disc. • Move the disc and encourage him to now take the takeout of your hand. • Once he has the concept, try throwing the disc in front of him and see if he goes after it. If he does, try increasing the distance. Now encourage him to catch it in midair, making sure you always throw low. • Once he has throwing down, try having him retrieve and bring back to you. You can use a long 30' tracking lead to encourage bringing it back. If your dog is already trained to come, you can easily encourage him to bring the disc back. ONLY have him come back WITH the disc. You may want to find another command associated with the disc. • You should also teach your dog the 'leave it' or 'drop it' command to have him release the disc. • Go to your local disc dog club to learn more advanced moves for Freestyle.

EQUIPMENT	EQUIPMENT - Great list of equipment found on **US Disc Dog National** - *https://usddn.com/* 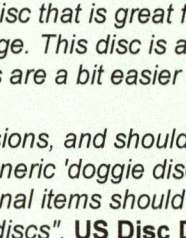
	
	 • **Disc**
	 Soft, light, thin material. Use discs that are made for canines. Other materials may be brittle and break with the dog possible ingesting. Sandpaper may be used to file down rough edges. Here are some examples listed on **US Disc Dog Nationals**
	 • **Floppy Disc**
	 A cloth/nylon disc with a rubber outer ring. Nice because they float!
	     ○ *These discs are very flexible, and some tricks that require a rigid disc are difficult to perform with them*
	 • **Nylabone**
	 These are closer to 'regulation' than Floppy Discs and are probably just as safe.
	     ○ *Be aware that there are some version of the Nylabone disc that are harder than others. Make sure you get the flexible, rubbery type.*
	     ○ *Note that there is a Gumabone model with a bone shape extending out of the top of the disc. While safe and easy for dogs to pick up, these discs fly like bricks.*
	 • **Frisbee Fastback**
	 This is the disc of choice for most Frisbee dog enthusiasts.
	     ○ *The Fastback Frisbee disc is a 107 gram disc made out of a soft PVC type plastic that a person can actually mar with a fingernail quite easily.*
	     ○ *They don't last as long as the harder types you can find in pet stores, but that means they are less damaging to the dog's teeth.*
	     ○ *The lightness of the Fastback allows it to remain aloft longer than most discs and therefore give its canine pursuer more time to catch it.*
	 • **Aerobie**
	 Aerobie discs come in three flavors: T
	     ○ *he **Aerobie Superdisc,** which is made from a transparent plastic with a soft rubber rim. This disc will fly a long ways, and is light enough and soft enough to be considered a good doggie disc;*
	     ○ *The **Aerobie Sprint** flying ring, made from a hard plastic coated with a softer rubber. While this ring can be used with dogs also, its low profile makes it easy to put a lot of velocity behind it, so use it for short tosses or long-distance throws, being careful to not throw it directly at your dog;*
	     ○ *Finally, the **Aerobie Jelly disc** is a flexible disc that is great for puppies or folks concerned about tooth wear and damage. This disc is a little more rigid than the Floppy Disc, so tricks like butterflies are a bit easier to perform.*
	 • **Other discs**
	 Any other discs used should be soft, have no protrusions, and should not be much heavier than 110 grams. In other words, the hard, generic 'doggie discs' one can sometimes find in pet stores or be given as promotional items should be avoided, as should 185-gram freestyle discs and especially golf discs". **US Disc Dog Nationals**
	 • **Protective Gear** (for you if dog is vaulting off your body):
	 Neoprene diving vest for the body; Thigh wrap for the legs; Waist wrap. Safety goggles.
	 • **Cones and Measuring Tape.**
	 To mark off distances.

TREIBBALL - 'Rolling sheep'	
BREED TYPE and/or BODY TYPE	Any breed can participate, but mainly created for herding dogs.
DESCRIPTION	This is a dog sport that was started in Germany and hit the mainstream as a sanctioned competition in 2008. <ul><li>The purpose of the game is to drive 8 45-75 cm exercise balls into a soccer sized goal using herding and obedience commands.</li><li>The off-leash dog must follow the handlers commands through whistles, verbal signals and/or hand signals to get the balls in into the goal within 10-15 minutes depending on the rules.</li><li>This is a great game that promotes teamwork and problem-solving skills, as the handler must direct the dog to push the ball with either his nose or shoulder in the order directed by ball size or color.</li><li>According to the American Treibball Association (ATA) this is a great sport for dogs that are shy, have impulse control, love to herd or are energetic.</li></ul>
PRECAUTIONS	See General Precautions and *Precautions* above in addition to following: Pushing on the box can put a lot of stress on the dog's wrist, especially in smaller dogs that need to put more pressure. <ul><li>Dogs usually turn in one direction, so it is important that you practice with your dog doing figure eights for example in the opposite direction. For example, if your dog always turns left, he can have cervical problems and tightened muscles on that side.</li><li>TMJ (Jaw) problems from grasping the ball with his mouth.</li><li>Other problems that can arise from this sport are problems with the lower back, back hock and iliopsoas.</li></ul>
TRAINING	This book is not on skills training, but here are a few things your dog should be able to do. <ul><li>Basic commands, such as sit, down, stay (for at least 5 seconds) and heel.</li><li>Target - he must be able to touch the ball with his nose and/or shoulder to drive the ball.</li><li>Learn commands off lead.</li></ul>
EQUIPMENT	EQUIPMENT <ul><li>Eight exercise balls - 45-75 cm depending on size of dog.</li><li>Soccer goal or equivalent</li><li>20 ft lead for distance work.</li></ul>

References

American Kennel Club https://www.akc.org/

LURE COURSING

American Kennel Club – Lure Coursing - https://www.akc.org/sports/coursing/lurecoursing/

American Kennel Club – Lure Coursing – Eligible Breeds https://www.akc.org/sports/coursing/lure-coursing/eligible-breeds/

American Sighthound Field Association https://asfa.org/coursing.htm

Irish Wolfhound Club of America https://iwclubofamerica.org/events

Wikipedia – Lure Coursing https://en.wikipedia.org/wiki/Lure_coursing

AGILITY

Agility (*Wikipedia*) https://en.wikipedia.org/wiki/Dog_agility

American Kennel Club – Agility - https://www.akc.org/sports/agility/

Zink, C and Daniels, J (2005). Jumping from A to Z.

Zink, C (2004). Peak Performance: Coaching the Canine Athlete.

FLYBALL

American Kennel Club – Flyball - https://www.akc.org/expert-advice/sports/flyball-101-how-to-compete-in-flyball-for-dogs/

Flyball (*Wikipedia*) https://en.wikipedia.org/wiki/Flyball

PetMD - Flyball - https://www.petmd.com/dog/general-health/flyball-for-dogs-an-ultimate-guide-for-your-athletic-pooch

DISC DOG

Disc Dog (Wikipedia); https://en.wikipedia.org/wiki/Disc_dog

US Disc Dog Nationals https://usddn.com/

HyperFlite https://hyperflite.com/discs-overview/

TREIBBALL

American Kennel Club – Treibball - https://www.akc.org/expert-advice/sports/treibball-this-sport-isnt-just-for-herding-breeds/

National Association of Treibball Enthusiasts - https://www.nationaltreibball.com/

Treibball: Give it a Try! - Karen Prior Clicker Training - https://clickertraining.com/treibball-give-it-a-try/

Swimming and Walking

The advantages of swimming are:
- On a regular basis, swimming can help build the endurance, muscle strength, flexibility, range of motion in joints and cardiovascular fitness.
- This is a great sport for all fitness levels.
- This can help in post-surgery to avoid muscle atrophy and weakness. Swimming is also good for people and pets that cannot do weight bearing activities – it provides unloading on painful joints, and early weight bearing.
- Swimming does not put the strain on connective tissues that running, aerobics and some weight-training routines do.
- Hydrotherapy on an underwater treadmill helps the canine with limb extension, where swimming does more to help flexion.

The advantages of walking:
- Whether you live in the city or country, there is usually a place that you can walk.
- Improves cardiovascular fitness.
- Walking helps with weight loss.
- Walking with your dog helps to build up your endurance, as most dogs will be more than happy to walk as far as you can tolerate.
- Walking helps increase bone density.
- It is a great way to burn off energy for your dog. A tired dog is a happy dog.
- Change of scenery for both you and your dog. Despite having a 'big' back yard or having a small dog in an apartment, most dogs get tired of looking at the same four walls. Walking your dog enhances their senses, helps them socially, and best of all gives them quality time with you. 30+ minutes a day also helps decrease depression in humans.

References and Reading/Websites

Breed Section

AKC (American Kennel Club)   www.akc.org

American Kennel Club (2006) *The Complete Dog Book, 20th Edition*. New York: Ballantine Books

Dogs USA Magazine (2005). *AKC Groups and Breeds,* pp 22-23. 20th Anniversary Collector's Edition, Vol. 20

Iams : https://www.iams.com/

Lost Temple Pets: www.losttemplepets.com

OFA - Orthopedic Foundation for Animals https://ofa.org/

Pugnetti, Gino (1980). *Simon & Schuster's Guide to Dogs.* New York: Simon and Schuster.

Wikipedia: http://en.wikipedia.org/wiki/List_of_dog_breeds. Most of the pictures for this book were retrieved by Wikipedia public domain .

Zink, Christine M (1997). *Peak Performances: Coaching the Canine Athlete, 2nd Edition.* Maryland: Canine Sports Production

Sport / Activity Section

Dog and Human Sports

Active Dog Sports - *Articles on Canicross, Bikejoring, Scootering, Skijoring, etc.*
https://activedogsports.com/category/dog-mushing/

American Kennel Club – *How to get Started in Canicross -*
https://www.akc.org/expert-advice/health/canicross-goes-beyond-running-with-dogs/

Canicross by Mike Callahan. Previously published in Mushing Magazine November/December 2001
http://www.skijor.com/canicross.html

Canicross USA - https://canicrossusa.org/

Doggie Sport - *Skijoring With Dogs | Getting Started, Equipment & Breeds!* by Sacha
Parent https://doggiesport.com/skijoring-with-dogs/

KUHL - *Feel the Pull: Dog Skijoring and Urban Mushing -*
https://www.kuhl.com/borninthemountains/dog- skijoring

MUSH! *A Beginner's Manual of Sled Dog Training,* by LaBelle, Charlene - editor for Sierra Nevada Dog
Drivers, Inc.

NEEWA - *What Is Bikejoring? The Ultimate Guide To Dog Bikejoring -*
https://www.neewadogs.com/pages/bikejoring

North American Canicross - https://nacanicross.com/

Rover.com (The Dog People) - *Skijoring is the Best Dog Sport You've Never Heard Of*
https://www.rover.com/blog/skijoring-dog-sport-skis/

Running Dogs (blog) http://skijorbikejorcanicross.blogspot.com/2008/05/equipment-needed-for-skijoring.html

Sled Dog Central http://www.sleddogcentral.com/skijorarticles.htm#introduction

Ski Spot Run by Haakenstad and Thompson for lots of information on skijoring and more.

SkiJor Now http://www.skijornow.com

Dog Pulling Sports

American Kennel Club - *Tips on Doing Advanced Drafting Work With Your Dog*
https://www.akc.org/expert-advice/training/doing-advanced-drafting-work/

Carting with your Dog http://www.cartingwithyourdog.com/cfaq.html#Commands

Fun with Draft by Phil Chagnon https://bmdcc.ca/

Iditarod – Official Site http://www.iditarod.com/learn/terminology.html

International Weight Pull Association http://www.iwpa.net/Rules.html

MUSH! *A Beginner's Manual of Sled Dog Training,* by LaBelle, Charlene - editor for Sierra Nevada Dog Drivers, Inc.

Ski Spot Run by Haakenstad and Thompson for lots of information on skijoring and more.

Snowpaw Store https://snowpawstore.com/collections/weight-pull

Tri-State Alaskan Malamute Club http://www.tsamc.org/forms/Rules.html

Wikipedia: Drafting - https://en.wikipedia.org/wiki/Drafting_(dog)

Wikipedia: Sled Dog http://en.wikipedia.org/wiki/Sled_dogs

Wikipedia: Sled Dog Racing http://en.wikipedia.org/wiki/Sled_dog_racing .

What is Pulka? *By Wise Geek* http://www.wisegeek.com/what-is-pulka.html

Instinct Sports

Acme Canine -Training A Dog To Track https://acmecanine.com/training-a-dog-to-track-slow-and-methodical-process/

American Breeder - *How do I train my dog to track scents?*
https://www.americanbreeder.com/resources/american-breeder-blog/dogs/dog-scent-tracking-training-guide

American Kennel Club (AKC): Earthdog https://www.akc.org/sports/earthdog/

American Kennel Club (AKC): Herding https://www.akc.org/sports/herding/

American Kennel Club (AKC): Tracking https://www.akc.org/sports/tracking/

Dirt Dog - AWTA https://www.awta.org/

Gundog - How to Train the Dual-Purpose Retriever
https://www.gundogmag.com/editorial/how-to-train-dualpurpose-retriever/466559

Gundog - *How To: Develop A Great Pointing Dog*
https://www.gundogmag.com/editorial/how-to-develop-a-great-pointing-dog/175551

Gundog - *A Balanced Approach to Training Your Flushing Dog*
https://www.gundogmag.com/editorial/balanced-approach-training-flushing-dog/367828

Hepper Blog - *How to Train a Dog to Track: 6 Vet-Approved Steps* - By Brooke Billingsley Updated on October 24, 2025 - https://articles.hepper.com/how-to-train-dog-to-track/

Magic's Legacy – Herding, Instinct Tests - https://www.shannonwolfeherding.com/instinct-tests

Mossy Oak - *Retriever Training and Hunting - How to Train*
By Bill Gibson, Head Trainer of Mossy Oak Gamekeeper Kennels
https://www.mossyoak.com/our-obsession/blogs/dogs/retriever-training-and-hunting-how-to-train

Wikipedia: Gun Dog https://en.wikipedia.org/wiki/Gun_dog

Wikipedia: Herding Dog https://en.wikipedia.org/wiki/Herding_dog

Water Sports

American Kennel Club - *Diving Dogs 101*- https://www.akc.org/expert-advice/sports/diving-dogs-101/

Dixie Dock Dogs https://www.dixiedockdogs.com/#/

Dock Dogs https://dockdogs.com/

Surf Dog Ricochet - *Teach your Dog to Surf* https://www.surfdogricochet.com/surfing-dogs-teach-your-dog-to-surf.html

Portuguese Water Dog Club of America's Water Trial Manual https://www.pwdca.org /

Newfoundland Club of America https://www.ncanewfs.org/index.html

North America Diving Dogs - https://northamericadivingdogs.com/

World Dog Surfing - https://www.surfdogchampionships.com/

Outdoor Sports

AKC – American Kennel Club - Hiking With Dogs: Tips For Hitting the Trail https://www.akc.org/expert-advice/lifestyle/tips-for-hiking-with-your-dog/

AKC – American Kennel Club - How to Kayak With Your Dog https://www.akc.org/expert-advice/health/how-to-kayak-with-your-dog/

Pets that Travel - Camping with Dogs: Ultimate Guide! https://www.petsthattravel.com/camping-with-dogs/

Rover.com - Dog Kayaks: A Guide to Kayaking with Your Dog (and Which Kayaks Are Best) https://www.rover.com/blog/dog-kayaks-a-guide-to-kayaking-with-your-dog-and-which-kayaks-are-best/

Tips for Hiking with your Dog by Hike with your dog http://www.hikewithyourdog.com/page156/page156.html

The Manuel: Take your Dog Hiking by Angele Sionna & Elisabeth Kwak-Hefferan for Backpacker https://www.backpacker.com/home

Protection Sports

All American K9: https://all-americank-9.com/

Canadian Ring Sport - The Basic Philosophy of Ring Sport by Jean-Michel Moreau & Chris Redenbach, 1991 https://www.canadianringsport.ca/philosophy-of-french-ring/

Dantero Malinois: https://dantero.com/articles/

K-9 Evolution - Mondio Ring https://k9evolutionsdogtraining.com/blog/all-about-mondio-ring/

Leeburg- The Exercises and Scores in the Belgium Ring By Germain Pauwels https://leerburg.com/bel-ring1.htm

North American Ring Association NARA: http://www.ringsport.org/index.php?pg=ringsport

Schutzhund Training. com https://schutzhund.uk/fullscreen/fullscreen-slideshow-2/

United Schutzhund Club of America https://www.germanshepherddog.com/about/schutzhund-training /

Wikipedia – Schutzhund - https://en.wikipedia.org/wiki/Schutzhund

Popular Sports

American Kennel Club https://www.akc.org/

LURE COURSING

American Kennel Club – Lure Coursing - https://www.akc.org/sports/coursing/lurecoursing/

American Kennel Club – Lure Coursing – Eligible Breeds https://www.akc.org/sports/coursing/lure-coursing/eligible-breeds/

American Sighthound Field Association https://asfa.org/coursing.htm

Irish Wolfhound Club of America https://iwclubofamerica.org/events

Wikipedia – Lure Coursing https://en.wikipedia.org/wiki/Lure_coursing

AGILITY

Agility (*Wikipedia*) https://en.wikipedia.org/wiki/Dog_agility

American Kennel Club – Agility - https://www.akc.org/sports/agility/

Zink, C and Daniels, J (2005). Jumping from A to Z.

Zink, C (2004). Peak Performance: Coaching the Canine Athlete.

References - Breed & Sport Section

FLYBALL

American Kennel Club – Flyball - https://www.akc.org/expert-advice/sports/flyball-101-how-to-compete-in-flyball-for-dogs/

Flyball (*Wikipedia*) https://en.wikipedia.org/wiki/Flyball

PetMD - Flyball - https://www.petmd.com/dog/general-health/flyball-for-dogs-an-ultimate-guide-for-your-athletic-pooch

DISC DOG

Disc Dog (Wikipedia); https://en.wikipedia.org/wiki/Disc_dog

US Disc Dog Nationals https://usddn.com/

HyperFlite https://hyperflite.com/discs-overview/

TREIBBALL

American Kennel Club – Treibball - https://www.akc.org/expert-advice/sports/treibball-this-sport-isnt-just-for-herding-breeds/

National Association of Treibball Enthusiasts - https://www.nationaltreibball.com/

Treibball: Give it a Try! - Karen Prior Clicker Training - https://clickertraining.com/treibball-give-it-a-try/

License, Certificates or Completed Courses

L/PTA – Physical Therapy Asst.

ACE Certified Personal Trainer

Dip. Canine Fitness/Nutrition

E-Training for Dogs:

Canine Genetics

Canine Fitness Program:
- All Fit Dog
- All Fit Puppy
- Athletic Performance Fitness Strategies

NC State Veterinary Medicine:

Canine Arthritis Management Practitioner (CAMP)

Advanced Coaptation for Companion Animals

C I: Certified Strength and Conditioning Coach (CSCC)

Certified Companion Animal Therapist (CCAT)
- C I: Introduction to Companion Animal Rehabilitation
- C II: Biophysical Agent Modalities and Therapeutic Exercises

www.ingramcontent.com/pod-product-compliance
Lightning Source LLC
Chambersburg PA
CBHW041141120626
46547CB00020B/3075